living treasures

CELEBRATION of the HUMAN SPIRIT

May 14, 2000
Dear Fred McCaffrey

Welcome to the Living Treasures
We hope you enjoy this book
for years to come.

All our best,
The Living Treasure Committee

Delfinio Lujan

living treasures

CELEBRATION OF THE HUMAN SPIRIT

A Legacy of New Mexico

Photography **JOANNE RIJMES**

Text **KAREN NILSSON BRANDT** & **SHARON NIEDERMAN**

Foreword **MARY LOU COOK**

WESTERN EDGE PRESS
Santa Fe

CLOUDS: Joanne Rijmes' clouds are used when the photograph of a Treasure is unavailable.

Published by Western Edge Press, 126 Candelario Street, Santa Fe, New Mexico 87501.

Library of Congress Catalog Card Number: 96-62011

ISBN 1-889921-00-9

Edited by Ann Mason
Design and production by Jim Mafchir, Western Edge Graphics
Calligraphy by Mary Lou Cook

Printed in Hong Kong

Contents

FOREWORD: In Praise of Elders   x
Mary Lou Cook

MUCHAS GRACIAS   viii
Acknowledgements

THE LIVING TREASURES:

HERMAN AGOYO   2
Serving New Mexico's Indian Pueblos

BILL ARAGON   4
A True Friend and Neighbor

JESUSITA ARAGON   6
From a Tradition of Healing and Birthing

HAZEL ARCHER   8
A Teacher of Perception

FATHER MIGUEL BACA   10
The City Different's Biker Priest

EMILY OTIS BARNES   12
Vintage Understanding and Friendship

ANN BARTH   14
Life Dedicated to Nursing

WINNIE BEASLEY   16
Motorcycle Mama

ROBERT BOISSIERE   18
Homo Spiritus

TRUMAN BRIGHAM   20
Organic Gardening Pioneer of Española

ELEANOR BROH-KAHN   22
New Mexico's Grant Maven

ANTHONY & GITA BROOKE   24
International Peace Networkers

ALICE BULLOCK   26
A Love of Words

JACQUES CARTIER   28
Fire Dancer Extraordinaire

MODESTA CHARLEY   30
Preserving Ceremonial Dress

MANUEL "BOB" CHAVEZ   32
Fulfilling a Promise to the Great Spirit

PEGGY POND CHURCH   34
A Passion for Poetry

WILLARD CLARK   36
Engraved in the Heart of Santa Fe

MARY LOU COOK   38
A Design for Life

HELEN CORDERO   40
Storyteller Creator

CORDELIA CORONADO   42
Weaver of Tradition

ANN DASBURG   44
Always Working for Peace

MARY WOODARD DAVIS   46
Textile Artist

STAN & ZU DAVIS   48
Town and Community Builders

CAROL DECKER   50
Promoting Respect for Cultural Differences

RAE DOUGLAS   52
Northern New Mexico's Christmas Lady

DORATHEA DUNAKIN   54
Watching Santa Fe Evolve

BERTHA DUTTON   56
Daughter of the Desert

BETTY EGAN   58
Madre of Rancho Encantado

RICHARD & JEAN ERDOES   60
Collaborators for Art and Justice

VIOLA FISHER   62
Angel of Cerro Gordo Park

MURRAY FRIEDMAN   64
Pioneer of Pain Control

EVE GENTRY   66
The Embodiment of Creative Vitality

PAULINE GOMEZ   68
Teacher with Special Sight

TELESFOR GOODMORNING   70
Raising Blue Corn and White Corn

SHIRLEY & MARY GREENE   72
*Ecclesiastical "Bureaucrat" &
Pioneer Woman Minister*

TINO GRIEGO   74
Coaching from a Wheelchair

JIM & RUTH HALL   76
Taking the Reins

ROSALIE HELLER   78
*Setting the Tone for Northern New
Mexico Music*

JOHN HIGHTOWER   80
Eliciting Trust at the Highest Level

ALLAN HOUSER   82
Father of Contemporary Indian Sculpture

HARMON & CORNELIA HULL   84
Building Community

BILL ISAACS   86
Advocate for Mother Nature

JOHN B. JACKSON   88
Geographer of the West

BILL & JULIE JAMES   90
Bringing People Together

MYRA ELLEN JENKINS   92
NewMexico's Historian

BERGERE KENNEY   94
Beloved Physician

JOHN KENNEY   96
Lover of the Land

ELEANOR KING   98
Grand Lady of Dance

NORBERT KREIDL   100
Expert in Glass Technology

JACK & MARGE LAMBERT   102
Explorers of Trails and Cultures

DELFINIO LUJAN   104
Master of Remedios

WILLIAM LUMPKINS   106
Artist, Architect, Activist

TOMMY MACAIONE   108
Painter, Politician, Pontificator

DOROTHY McKIBBIN   110
Gatekeeper of Los Alamos

VIRGINIA MACKIE   112
A Profound Love of Music

TONA & ELIAS MAES   114
Leaders of the Grand March

JOHN MANLEY   116
Influencing the Course of History

PEACH MAYER   118
The First Lady of Opera

FAITH MEEM   120
The Spirit of Civility

SENSEI NAKAZONO   122
Natural Healing Practitioner

ROSE NARANJO   124
Potter and Matriarch

LLOYD KIVA NEW   126
Turning Traditional Crafts into New Art Forms

BEAUMONT NEWHALL   128
Author of the History of Photography

BEN ORTEGA   130
Searching for Leña

ALFONSO ORTIZ   132
Activist Anthropologist

HAZEL PARCELLS   134
Healing Pioneer

POLLY PATRAW   136
A Grand Canyon Life

RHEUA PEARCE   138
Living the Creative Process

MEL PFAELZER   140
Supporter of Education and the Arts

MAGGIE PHINNEY   142
Volunteerism as a Profession

EDITH PIERPONT   144
Protector of the Environment

PAULINE POLLOCK   146
Plaza Retailer

JUAN QUINTANA   148
Grateful amidst Adversity

TONY REYNA   150
Service to Pueblo and Nation

GREGORITA RODRIGUEZ   152
Curandera

HELENE RUTHLING   154
From the Black Forest to Tesuque

AMALIA SANCHEZ   156
First Fiesta Queen

GLORIA SAWTELL   158
Indefatigable Volunteer

JAY SCHERER   160
Selfless Healer and Teacher

SCORE   162
Guiding New Businesses

BOUNCER SENA   164
An Abiding Belief in Kids

PHIL SHULTZ   166
Mender of Broken Wings

CAROL & MARCUS SMITH   168
Dedicated Doctors

MYRTLE STEDMAN   170
Adobe Artist

JOHN STEPHENSON   172
Feeding the Multitudes

BOB STOREY   174
Interviewing as Art

ANITA GONZALES THOMAS   176
Preserving Spanish Colonial New Mexico

FRANCES TYSON   178
Energy Saver

PABLITA VELARDE   180
Artist Who Led the Way

CHARLIE & DOROTHY WADE   182
Making Music and Creating Gardens

SALLIE WAGNER   184
Guardian of Cultural Heritage

CORINNE WOLFE   186
Lobbying for Human Rights

K. ROSE WOOD   188
Advocate for Seniors

THANK YOU   191
List of Donors

FOREWORD: In Praise of Elders

MARY LOU COOK

SINCE 1984, WHEN THE NETWORK FOR THE COMMON GOOD began its work in Santa Fe, we have honored one hundred ten remarkable older citizens of northern New Mexico, as Living Treasures—surgeons and shopkeepers, pueblo governors, archaeologists, musicians, midwives, environmentalists and farmers. This book, our first, introduces one hundred four of our beloved elders, in Joanne Rijmes' skillful, sensitive photo essays, with accompanying texts by Sharon Niederman and Karen Nilsson Brandt.

Taken together, these brief biographies form an intimate and lively composite portrait of what has been called "the civic generation"—men and women born between 1900 and 1920, for the most part, survivors of the Depression and the Second World War, great joiners, organizers, community activists. They volunteered with the PTA, the Republican and Democratic Parties, the Sierra Club, the League of Women Voters. They gave us the environmental movement, the peace movement, good schools, the beginnings of alternative health care.

This book is full of pioneer women: Modesta Charley, of San Juan pueblo, was one of the first pueblo women to receive a higher education. Polly Patraw was one of the first women naturalist/park rangers. Mary Greene was one of the first women ministers ordained in the Congregational Church. Ann Dasburg opened a racially integrated day care center in the early 1940s. Cornelia Hull, in the same era, created the first community effort on behalf of Mexican-American migrant workers in the U.S.

You'll meet Dr. Marcus Smith, one of the first American physicians to enter Dachau after the German surrender in 1945; sculptor Allan Houser, the first native American to win the National Medal of Arts; Sensei Nakazono, the acupuncturist who did more than anyone to legitimize alternative therapies in New Mexico and the country as a whole.

And they did it all quietly, no fuss, no publicity. Modesty is a recurring theme in these pages. Rose Naranjo, master potter of Sta Clara Pueblo takes no credit for her art. "Clay will form itself into what clay wants to be." Delfinio Lujan, who pre-scribed healing herbs to generations of Santa Feans from his shop on Galisteo Street, liked to say "I'm a merchant, not a healer;the herbs do that." Pulitzer Prize journalist John Hightower bluepencilled his editorials *after* they had run, still searching for a better turn of phrase.

The other striking quality in these lives is a reverent atten-tiveness to the world, openness, receptivity, kindness. "It's wonderful to learn to watch without judgment and opinion," says photographer Hazel Archer. "We must learn to look with-out judgment, " agrees James Brinkerhoff Jackson,the geogra-pher who put landscape studies into the university curricu-lum. Bill Aragon, builder and community activist, puts it this way. "Your friend doesn't have to live like you do, but if you show him respect,he'll show you respect." Wisdom without preaching is the core of this book.

Santa Fe, despite enormous changes in recent years, is still the City Different. Use this book as guide to the city's architec-ture (William Lumpkins and historic preservation), its musical summers (Bergere Kenney and the Chamber Music Festival), the Farmers' Market (passionate gardener Truman Brigham) and of course Fiesta (Amalia Sanchez, our first Fiesta Queen). And you'll find dozens of stories of Santa Fe the way it used to be.

Living Treasures is one of those simple ideas you wish you'd thought of sooner. In spring 1984, a group of us in Santa Fe realized we were tired of protest, against the ballooning arms budget, against talk of winnable nuclear wars, against attacks on welfare mothers. We longed to be *for* something. We had in mind Gandhi's advice, "You must be the change you wish to see in the world."

It didn't take long to find what we were all in favor of: members of the older generation who had made a difference. Our elders, living longer than ever before in human history, and doing so with grace and spirit and undiminished energy for good works. But all of them somehow off to one side, marginalized in our country, that values youth, power, novelty. Our winner take all society awards few prizes to men and women in their seventies and eighties.

It wasn't that way in other cultures, we knew. In the pueblos of New Mexico, the elders are the bearers of tradition, religious belief and native language. In New Mexico Hispanic culture, the extended family is paramount. Grandparents get respect. In Asian cultures too, the elders are heeded. A Japanese tradition of honoring folk artists gave us the model for Living Treasures

Twice a year, in spring and fall, we honor three older New Mexicans. When we phone to tell them they've been named Living Treasures, they invariably protest, with typical modesty, "Why me? I don't deserve it. Others have done a whole lot more." Never mind, we treat them like celebrities. Celebrity is strenuous: we ask them to submit to a long interview — an oral history—which is taped and archived at the Santa Fe Public Library. Photographer Joanne Rijmes spends hours, sometimes all day, with each Living Treasure. Her incomparable photographs were the inspiration for this book. Its text is drawn from the taped histories in our archive.

We fete our Living Treasures at a simple ceremony to which the whole town is invited. No pomp and circumstance, we sit in a circle and reminisce. Friends and neighbors of the honorees tell old, forgotten stories. We laugh, we're moved to tears. Reverence is not required. This event is part tribute, part gentle send-up. At times it's a class reunion, as when Robert Chavez' former pupils —the artists, athletes, teachers he gave their start in life—showed up en masse to thank him. At times, it's a living memorial.

After everyone else has spoken, our Living Treasures respond with a little speech or story. Our formerly small town —now grown in some respects beyond recognition — shrinks back to human size. The ceremony strengthens old ties and creates new ones. It binds up the community.

The Living Treasures idea has taken hold in New Mexico. The city of Taos and Rio Arriba County have adopted it. Nationally, Denville, New Jersey, Ogden, Utah, Sedona, Arizona have come up with their own versions. As for us, we're still improvising. We make rules and break rules. Lately we've branched out into the schools, encouraging children to learn history from their grandparents and other seniors. In our sixth year, we planted thirty-six trees—honoring thirty-six Living Treasures—in a local park.

And we've gathered the first ten years of Living Treasures into this book, full of surprises. One is its sheer reach in time. Our elders remember grandparents and grandchildren and give us a multigenerational saga. The whole century is here: Geronimo's surrender, the Bataan Death March, the Manhattan Project, the founding of the UN, the Bicentennial. But also — that's the beauty of oral history—births, deaths, marriages, gardens, picnics, banjos, motorcycles, private life and public service. Who are we? Where are we going? What do we owe ourselves and others? This book, this chorus of voices asks a bunch of salutary questions. Beyond the wisdom of individual lives, it offers the collective wisdom of a generation.

Thank you Joanne Rijmes—

    for extraordinary gifts

    for making visible simplicity,

      grace and deep goodness,

    for sourcing heart and soul,

    for old memories of kinship, and

    for communicating with clouds

MUCHAS GRACIAS

ACKNOWLEDGMENTS

Past and Present Committee Members since 1984

Anna Bryson
James Baker
Susan Boyle
Mike Boyle
Anthony Brooke
Gita Brooke
Barbara Conroy
Kate Cook
Courtney Cook
Mary Lou Cook
Kate Cochrane
Dorothy Calcott
Margo Covington
David Cunningham
Ann Dasburg
Nancy Dahl
Anne Hays Egan
Marilyn Gatlin
George Greer
Megan Harris
Bob Harris
Phil Howell
Allan Hutner
Marcia Keegan
Nancy Kenney
Denise Kusel
Nance López
Ramón López

Allen Jay Lerner
Dennis Liddy
Barbara Mallery
Barbara Marigold
Jennifer Minett
Shirley Minett
Barbara Murphy
Bill Paiss
Charles Purdy
Dorothy Perron
Bernadette Parnell
Louise Ramberg
Joanne Rijmes
Ramona Sakiestewa
Sarai Saporta
Mary Schultz
Jane Shea
Katherine Shelton
Carolyn Silver
Carol Steiro
Bob Storey
Rina Swentzel
Nancy Terry
Kathryn Tillson
Sherry Wallace
Martha Walter
Chet Watson
Laney Watson
Yvonne Wilson
Zemmie Wimmett

Pro Bono Support

Eleanor Morris Caponigro
Kay Carlson
Norma Evans
Pat French
Gil Frith
Eloyse Garthwaite
Eric and Elise Gent
Cullen Hallmark
Anne Hillerman
Cynthia Jones
Judith Liersch
Lynn Lown
Joe and Debra Roberts
Suzanne Ruta
Valdes Art Supply

McCune Charitable Foundation
for their exceedingly generous support

Family and Friends
of the Living Treasures, who gave of their time to make the writing possible.

Special Donors

The names of donors of one thousand dollars appear on the pages of their chosen Treasures.

living treasures

CELEBRATION of the HUMAN SPIRIT

Herman Agoyo

SERVING NEW MEXICO'S INDIAN PUEBLOS

"I THINK BEING INVOLVED in sports opened a lot of doors—to education—to recognition—to travel," said Herman Agoyo of San Juan Pueblo. "My dream was to play professional baseball."

Born at the Santa Fe Indian Hospital in 1934, Herman grew up with his "grandpa and Aunt Juanita." He had "no education and didn't really promote education" because the mindset of the times was that Indians should learn a vocational skill. "That was drilled into the system at Santa Fe Indian School, too, because educators basically all the way from Washington on down saw the Indian people as being good with their hands. There was an emphasis on art and various vocational trades."

But Herman had other ideas. In the 1950s, the teachers at the Santa Fe Indian School didn't encourage students to go to college, he said. "By the time you reached ninth grade, you had to make a choice of what vocation you were going to specialize in. Some of us weren't interested in that. We wanted to go to college. . . . As I look back, I'm very grateful that the principal and some of the teachers listened to what we were saying. We asked for chemistry, foreign language, and typing."

When Herman was in ninth grade, he met Father Joel Byrne. After Father Joel was transferred to New Orleans, he continued to correspond with Herman, and recommended that he attend Manhattan College. Herman packed his bags for New York City—the only student from his fifty-four-member class at Santa Fe Indian School to go directly to a four-year college. He graduated from Manhattan College in 1958.

"I've been involved in earning a living in Indian affairs since 1965," Herman said. "It was the dream of Kennedy, but after his death it was President Johnson who implemented what we now know as the Great Society programs and the War on Poverty. Arizona State [University] got a contract to hire people like me to go into the Indian communities to tell them about the law and how to start community action programs. That was my job. Up to that point the only government agency we had dealt with was the Bureau of Indian Affairs. This opened the door to work with all federal agencies, which we are doing today."

Herman has served in many capacities in tribal and inter-tribal government. He became executive director of the Eight Northern Indian Pueblos Council at San Juan Pueblo but resigned in 1980 to take on the responsibility of coordinating the commemoration of the three hundredth anniversary of the 1680 Pueblo Revolt. "It was especially important to me because the principal leader of the revolt, Popé, was from San Juan Pueblo," Herman said.

In 1986, Herman was elected chairman of the All Indian Pueblo Council. In 1991 and 1993 he again served as executive director of the Eight Northern Indian Pueblos Council. In 1992 he was governor of San Juan Pueblo.

"I feel very fortunate that there is a program here that can keep me at home to be of service to the people, but at the same time also be involved in our cultural way of life here at the pueblo," he said. "It has been a very rewarding life. My grandpa raised me. I've helped raise my grandson. . . . It goes full circle."

"I think it's important for young people to be proud as Indians. In my own experience it was downplayed. . . . Our identity, our culture was ignored."   —*Herman Agoyo*

Bill Aragon

A TRUE FRIEND AND NEIGHBOR

BILL ARAGON GRADUATED FROM HIGH SCHOOL in the mining town of Silverton, Colorado in 1925. There were five girls and two boys in his graduating class. Unbeknownst to the two boys, the district named them as rival candidates for West Point. When Bill found out, he took himself out of the running. "It would take an extra bunch of money I didn't have," he recalled. And his big family, with two ailing sisters, needed him. With typical good will, he raised money to send his class-mate to the Academy.

Solidarity or simply friendship, he'd call it, has always been his guiding principle, a beacon to his neighbors on Santa Fe's west side. He came through town for the first time in 1931, after several years in the Colorado mines. He was on his way to Arizona, when he ran into the foreman of the Terrero mine (above Pecos) in a Santa Fe restaurant and was offered a job. "Great news! We'd made Santa Fe," was his reaction.

In Terrero, "we were a bunch of friends working together." When the United Mine Workers organized in Madrid and Terrero, Bill was for the union. He served on the grievance committee, and when the strike began in 1936, he walked the picket line, "rough nights out in that cold." His first child was born that year, in a one room shack on company land. American Metals hired a union buster. When the union tri-umphed at the end of a long strike, they shut down the mines in 1938.

By then Bill, "who knew how to carpenter a bit" had moved to Santa Fe to help a cousin build his house. A furniture company hired him as a door to door salesman. "My shoes are still all right; they'll last," he assured his employer. Later he worked, for better pay, with Charles Ilfeld's wholesale grocery.

The Depression lingered. "Rents were going up and wages weren't too good," so Bill set out to find a place of his own. With a loan of $300 from a local bank — his honesty the only collateral — he bought a "two room adobe shack," and "that's where I am right now. This is where I made my home sweet home. My neighborhood on the sunny side of Santa Fe."

Wartime brought work at Bruns Army Hospital and Los Alamos National Labs. Throughout it all Bill practised solidar-ity. When fire destroyed homes in his west side neighborhood, he organized friends to rebuild them. "I helped when help was needed. I always tried to be a good neighbor. I know a lot of people and I try to help them out in every way I can. We called it good community relations," he reflects on the spirit of mutu-al aid he promoted.

Because he practises what he preaches, Bill's advice rings true. And more apt it couldn't be in today's world. "Show friendship; show respect, and be helpful. When you do that, you're doing something. Your friend doesn't have to live like you do. But if you show him respect, he'll show you respect." Amen.

"I just decided I
would live my
life in a friendly
way."

—*Bill Aragon*

Jesusita Aragon

FROM A TRADITION OF HEALING AND BIRTHING

Doña Jesusita, healer and midwife of northern New Mexico, in her seven decades of on the job delivered more than twelve thousand babies—the population of a good sized New Mexican town. Born on a ranch in Sapello, known as El Rancho Trujillo, in 1908, she delivered her first baby when she was only thirteen years old. "My grandmother, Dolores Gallegos, a midwife, taught me," Jesusita recalled. "She wasn't there that day because she went to deliver another baby. One of my aunts had a baby, so I had to help her. But I knew everything."

Her Tía Valentina, the *curandera* in the family, taught her the use of traditional healing herbs. Jesusita became interested in healing as well as delivering babies.

"I wanted to go to school to be a nurse," said Jesusita. "But years ago, they didn't believe in education. I only went to the eighth grade, and it was all in Spanish. It's a miracle that I can talk a little English. I learned reading the papers."

As a single mother with a son and daughter, she was sole provider for her family. She cut wood and carried it to build her own house as well as the furnishings. She cared for her family by gardening and raising animals. In 1942 she moved to Las Vegas, where she supported her children by washing clothes, cleaning houses, making tortillas, and delivering babies.

The birthing room she set up in the front of her house held ten beds. "I used to deliver nine or ten a night," she recalled, charging $10 a birth. "I used to deliver 200 to 215 a year." Among her deliveries were twenty-seven sets of twins and two sets of triplets.

"Never mind how the baby comes," her grandmother told her. "Sometimes it's in the wrong position. Be patient. Don't let your lady know. She told me: 'Don't get nervous. Be silent.' Everything she taught me, happened. Some day, she said, a baby's gonna talk to you."

Blessed with good health and strong energy, Jesusita, the eldest of eight sisters, survived all her siblings. "I've never been sick," she said. Eventually, when she was in her eighties, a stroke forced her into retirement. "God does everything for me, that's how I feel. When I touch people, they feel better 'cause they trust me. You see, I just use my hands and my mind—and God."

"I bet you I can
deliver a baby in
the dark. I feel
everything with
my hands."

—*Jesusita Aragon*

Hazel Archer

A TEACHER OF PERCEPTION

"WATCHING HAS ALWAYS BEEN a part of my life. I don't know why," said Hazel Archer. "I was always more interested in watching what was going on. . . . When I began photographing, I was the observer."

Born in 1921 in Milwaukee, Wisconsin, to Chris and Ella Larsen, Hazel grew up with two brothers and a sister. At age ten she contracted polio. "I was fortunate to have such a supportive family," she recalls. "They encouraged me. Milwaukee had a very good homebound school program," which she attended until high school. "In high school, I started on braces and crutches." But although her activities were restricted, she developed keen powers of observation as a result.

After graduating from the University of Wisconsin, Hazel "happened to notice a few short little paragraphs in a Milwaukee paper about this summer school. One of my former teachers from Milwaukee was going to be there for a few weeks." Hazel applied. "Unbeknownst to me, a blessed star fell on my head," she said. German artist Josef Albers had assembled "this incredible faculty" at Black Mountain College, the renowned experimental arts institution in North Carolina.

At Black Mountain College Hazel studied photography. The college didn't have a degree program. "When the faculty saw an outstanding student who was very well qualified, the student would be accepted for graduation by an examiner."

There she met Buckminster Fuller and "photographed him a lot. We became good friends. He built his first dome ever at Black Mountain. He took me up in a small plane to photograph his dome."

Later, Hazel taught at Black Mountain, where she met her husband, Charles Archer. He had contracted tuberculosis in Japan during World War II, and came to North Carolina to recuperate. Hazel met him in a photography class. After they married, "the college began to disintegrate. We moved to the village of Black Mountain, started a photography studio, and became parents to Erika."

They moved to Tucson, Arizona, where Hazel founded two private schools—Hidden Springs and Avalon—because she "felt so strongly," and still does, "about the education of young children."

Hazel arrived in Santa Fe in the mid-1970s, lived on Canyon Road, and taught perception classes to adults and children. "I usually introduce the perception class by particular words that I find can bring about enfoldment," she said. "Perception is hard to describe, but it's wonderful to learn to watch without judgment and opinion. That which was not recognized previously begins to surface as some kind of surprise, and one begins to become aware of what one was not aware of previously."

Hazel's students learned about the "Big Four": Krishnamurti, Maria Montessori, Buckminster Fuller, and British spiritual leader Joel Goldsmith. "Because of their love, they were able to discern something on another wavelength that a child was expressing, while the child was being totally misunderstood by the adult," said Hazel. In 1989, she returned to Tucson, where she has taught classes in perception and design, and has been writing and working with her photographs. Her work—portraits primarily—has been exhibited at the Museum of Modern Art.

"To be with a group of people who are exploring is a wonderful way to live."   —*Hazel Archer*

Father Miguel Baca

THE CITY DIFFERENT'S BIKER PRIEST

"SANTA FE IS PART OF MY ESSENCE," Father Miguel Baca liked to say. And he was part of the essence of Santa Fe. When, after ordination in Indiana, he returned home to celebrate Mass for the first time at San Miguel—the oldest church in Santa Fe—Fray Angelico Chavez, the revered historian, was present to point out that in five hundred years of Spanish American Catholicism, Father Miguel was the first native-born Santa Fean to become a priest.

To be a priest means leaving home. Father Miguel left many times, and returned many times, always making his mark. He grew up in the heart of Santa Fe. His father was born where the Plaza restaurant now stands. Father Miguel, born 1927, was raised on Delgado Street. He belonged to the St Francis Cathedral parish. "Santa Fe was a closely-knit family-type community where everybody knew everybody,"he remembered. Going to church on Sunday was "part of existence, part of life."

His birth name was Arsenio. "I didn't like it," he recalled."Now I think it's a lovely name. When I entered into religious life I took the name Miguel—Michael—because Saint Michael is a hero of mine. "

Father Miguel went from grade school right to a seminary preparatory school in Cincinnati, Ohio. "I knew what I wanted from the very beginning. Since I can remember, all I ever wanted to be was—a Franciscan priest."

Five years after he was ordained he was assigned to a mission band, priests designated to go out and preach the gospel. "That's what I've been doing ever since," he told us, "travelling and preaching....almost a circuit rider....I've had a lot of experiences in Latin America, all over the U.S."

Pain accompanied his life. A car accident in the 1960s left him paralyzed. He fought persistently to regain the use of his legs. Within two years he was able to walk again, but the pain remained. "Pain has been a constant in my life," he said, looking back, "a good educator. I believe pain is worth something, if only to make you more sympathetic with people in pain. Pain is a very common thing in our existence."

In the mid 1980s he roared back into town on his Honda Goldwing. The "Biker priest" as he came to be known, befriended fellow bikers and invited members of the Northern New Mexico Bikers Association to distribute gifts to underprivileged children, and to provide labor for the restoration of San Lorenzo Church, in Picuris Pueblo.

San Lorenzo "was falling down, the fate of all those old adobes," Father Miguel recalled. "I rounded up the bikers in Santa Fe. I'd take them up to Picuris. We'd go up every Saturday for four years. We made over 30,000 adobes. We worked hard, laid the adobes, did a lot of plastering."

And then he left again. But in all his travels, he " never lost touch with Santa Fe.....Santa Fe has never left me," he affirmed. It never will. It's my town. I love it."

"I'm a connector.

I connect people.

It has been sort

of a theme in my

life."

—*Father Miguel Baca*

Emily Otis Barnes

VINTAGE UNDERSTANDING AND FRIENDSHIP

As a little girl, the first time she saw New Mexico Emily Otis Barnes said to herself: "This is where I shall live someday." Then, in 1927 she came west to visit her brother, the writer Raymond Otis. Through him, she met Mabel Dodge Luhan, Witter Bynner, and other writers and artists of the era. "I loved them," she said, and through meeting them, "doors flew open in all directions, and they became my friends, too."

Born in 1906 in Evanston, Illinois, Emily lived her early life in Chicago. But starting at age nine, her father, a director of the Santa Fe Railroad, took her out of school to travel with him, in his private car on inspection trips to the Southwest, up through California, and into Canada.

When the Depression came, her family's life changed. "Father lost a great deal, though not everything," she recalled. With little money, she and her new husband, architect Nathaniel Owings, who helped design the Chicago World's Fair, decided to go around the world. "We found a way to travel on freighters, on standby. We never knew what boat we were going to get on." The ten-month trip led them through the Orient, on second-class trains across India, from pension to pension, carrying their food. "It was an extraordinary journey," she remembered.

In another of her adventures, Emily "went down Wolf Creek Pass without brakes—and lived."

In 1944 she and her husband came to live in Santa Fe. They bought land and built a house in Pojoaque, where they raised their family of four children. "There were maybe nine thousand people here then. It was very beautiful and simple," she said.

In the late 1960s Emily went to New York to seek what her children called "her late blooming fortune." With Margaret Mead and editor Norman Cousins, she promoted an "interesting but rather vast" scheme for global cultural exchanges, International Cooperation Year. The President's wife took an interest. Emily and two hundred others were invited to a White House conference. Lunch with Lady Bird Johnson was lovely, but "there were no results."

The Wheelwright Museum, designed by Emily's friend William Penhallow Henderson, drew her into an enduring commitment. She calls the museum "my beloved place to be. In a way, it is my own temple." She was president of the board at the Wheelwright from 1983-85, executive secretary of the Southwest Association on Indian Affairs from 1971-76.

Although raised in the Episcopalian Church, Emily became a lifelong spiritual seeker, influenced first by her father, who through his travels became interested in Native American spirituality, and later, by her brother, who died at age thirty-eight.

"I seem to be a seeker in fields of all religions. I am moved by the Indians and by the Buddhists. The spiritual path is one you can take in all directions."

It is that sustaining spirituality, with its zest for exploration of different paths, that has guided her. "It's love and a wish for understanding," she remarked. "That's how I first got involved with the Wheelwright.

"I go through life a little bit on the fringe, led only by a simple-minded love of what's going to happen tomorrow. Now I am in my vintage years—and so I go forward."

"Each experience is an arrow guiding the way."   —*Emily Otis Barnes*

Ann Barth

LIFE DEDICATED TO NURSING

Born Anna Masterpole in Oelwein, Iowa, in 1911, Anna Barth preferred to be called Ann. She grew up in a family of seven. Her parents were Italian immigrants, and her father worked as a boilermaker for the Chicago Great Western Railroad.

Oelwein "was a railroad town with a population of about 10,000," according to Al Barth, Ann's husband, who also hailed from Oelwein. "We were born just a few weeks apart."

Ann's mother stayed home, but she enjoyed crocheting, and "she practically made them a living with her handiwork," Al said. Oelwein "was a small town, and everybody knew everybody. In high school, there was the usual rivalry in football between the Catholic high school that Ann attended and the public high school that I attended," Al remarked.

Al left school to go to work at age fourteen, and fifteen years passed before Ann saw him again. Ann had always wanted to be a nurse, but "the Depression came, and there was no money," Despite these hardships, Ann "worked for one year at the Oelwein Chemical Company, and she saved enough money to start her nurse's training in Des Moines, Iowa, at Mercy Hospital. She graduated in three years" and continued to work at Mercy.

When World War II began, Ann left Des Moines to work in Chicago at a hospital for marines. In February 1943, the Coast Guard sent Ann to Santa Fe "to open a hospital at the Japanese-American internment camp," Al said. At the time, both Ann and Al were corresponding separately with a friend from Oelwein who was living in California. The friend told Al that Ann was living in Santa Fe, and wrote Ann that her friend from Oelwein was living in Albuquerque—stationed at the Albuquerque Air Base, now Kirtland Air Force Base.

One day "Ann called me up and asked when I would have a day off," Al reminisced. She visited him in Albuquerque and invited him to come to Santa Fe when he had a pass.

The Barths were married in Santa Fe on August 16, 1944, in the chapel at Bruns Army Hospital. They had planned to return to Iowa, but Al found a job in Santa Fe and Ann went to work in a doctor's office until her only child, Bob, was born in 1947. She stayed home until Bob started school. Before she could return to work, however, Ann had to learn to drive. "She had never driven a car," said Al.

Ann worked at St. Vincent Hospital, the Santa Fe Indian Hospital, and the Santa Fe School for the Deaf, where she received an award for "never missing a night." She worked the night shift from 11 P.M. to 7 A.M..

Ann loved music. Although she never received formal musical training, she loved to play the piano and organ. She could hear a song and play it back perfectly. Ann played piano for the Silver Notes, a local group of senior musicians who performed for senior citizens groups and at nursing homes.

"Ann always
knew she wanted
to be a nurse."
—Al Barth
describing his wife,
Ann Barth

Winnie Beasley

MOTORCYCLE MAMA

THE HISTORY OF AVIATION is full of glamorous women. In the early decades there were Amelia Earhart, Beryl Markham, Winnie Beasley.

From the time Winabelle Rawson Pierce experienced her first airplane ride at age eleven, she wanted to become a pilot. Born in Des Moines, Iowa, and raised in Boston, she received her education at Bryn Mawr and Wellesley. Following college graduation, she attended Katherine Gibbs Secretarial School, but she held on to the dream she'd had since she was a girl.

Winnie enrolled in Lincoln Aviation Flying School in Nebraska, then went back home to live so she could save the money she needed to earn her pilot's license. Eventually, she went to Sioux Falls, South Dakota, where she received her private license. Then, with a $1,000 loan she bought a ten-year-old monocoup she called "Nellie." After receiving her commercial license and instructor's rating, she took off for Texas to seek her fortune as a flying instructor.

Stopping for a refueling in Blackwell, Oklahoma, Winnie was immediately hired as a flight instructor. Following a stormy period there, she moved to New York City to work for an airplane manufacturer. Not surprisingly, she convinced her boss to let her pick up and deliver airplanes from a factory in Orlando, Florida.

Then, in 1940, along with all licensed women commercial pilots, Winnie received a letter from Jacqueline Cochran asking her to join the Royal Air Force. Winnie answered the call. In Montreal, she passed the RAF test and she shipped out on a coal freighter for England. During the twenty-eight days aboard the ship, she learned to play poker, becoming expert enough to beat the captain.

Once overseas, she joined the Women's Air Transport Auxiliary and ferried planes from the United States to Scotland and fighter and bomber bases in England. She also flew British-built planes from factories to bases around the nation, including B-25 bombers. During the war, she met and fell in love with Colonel Peter Beasley. They married. She was twenty-eight; he was fifty-six.

Following the war, Winnie returned to the States, this time to Las Vegas, New Mexico, to look for a ranch to purchase. She worked as a reporter for the *Las Vegas Daily Optic.* Eventually, she and her husband moved to Tesuque, where they raised a family of four sons. Following the death of her husband in 1957, she remarried, but divorced after about a decade.

Known as "quite a character," Winnie could be seen riding her sidesaddle motorcycle, a replica of the one she drove during the war, around the streets of Santa Fe. Often she could be found in the town's nightspots, playing the gutbucket. A great horse lover, she started the Tesuque Hunt Club and taught many locals how to ride English style. She was a dog lover; her dogs garnered many blue ribbons. In addition, Winnie was a promoter of the arts, remembered for her contributions to the Santa Fe Opera and the Santa Fe Community Theater, where she helped with costumes, tickets, and even took part in productions.

"Mother Beasley," as she was affectionately nicknamed, was known as someone who could be counted on to help people when they first came to town, and she delighted in finding newcomers jobs and places to stay.

"Life begins at
sixty!"
—*Winnie Beasley*

Robert Boissiere

HOMO SPIRITUS

CROSSING THE ENORMOUS DISTANCE in miles and between cultures, Robert Boissiere followed his lifelong fascination with Native American people. He lived on the Hopi Reservation in the Arizona desert. By his seventies, the Frenchman was able to say he was "more Hopi than white man." His search for his "missing" Indian self led him to become an intermediary between the Indian and non-Indian worlds.

Born in Paris in 1914, Robert was educated as a lawyer and twice decorated for valor while serving with the French Army in World War II. During the war, he was taken prisoner by the Germans but escaped after a year and a half. He headed west in 1946, as soon as the war ended.

As a child in France, Robert had dreamed of American Indians, read everything he could find, and dressed in a Sioux "costume" at family gatherings. Later, while living in San Francisco he met Paul Coze, the French consul in Phoenix, an artist, and an authority on Southwest Indians. Coze invited him to serve as cook on an art expedition to Hopi. When the trip ended, Robert stayed on; he simply "didn't want to come back." Arriving there "it immediately felt like coming home." Robert ended up living with a Hopi family for two years, beginning to learn the Hopi way.

The author of several books on Hopi religion, culture, and folklore, including *Meditations with the Hopi* and *The Hopi Way: An Odyssey*, Robert says, "I wanted from the start to become native myself. I didn't want to change them, I didn't want to teach them. I wanted to be a member of a family."

In 1951, he married a Taos Pueblo woman, Mary Santanita Romero, and went to live at Taos Pueblo. Later on, he became known as the proprietor of Chez Robert, a restaurant in Cuyamungue. In 1991, he was part of the entourage of the Dalai Lama on his visit to Santa Fe.

As an author and teacher steeped in Native American tradition, Robert developed his philosophy that our species is evolving from "homo sapiens to homo spiritus."

"As I began to study what was possibly going on with today's society. I realized that we are involved in a decisive change in our way of life, what the Hopis call a purification time."

"I think the present-day society should feel proud of being involved in these tremendous changes, which I believe will eventually lead to a renewed and much more spiritual life than we have now."*

---

* From an article by Gussie Fauntleroy, *New Mexican*, n.d.

"From early childhood on, I had a constant feeling I belonged somewhere else beside France. I had the feeling that somehow I'd been an Indian."

—*Robert Boissiere*

Truman Brigham

ORGANIC GARDENING PIONEER OF ESPAÑOLA

Living off what the land can be coaxed to yield became a way of life for Truman Brigham early on. The first president of the Santa Fe Area Farmers Market was born in rural Arkansas on a "rock pile cotton farm." After two years of high school, he left home in search of a better life and landed in Clovis, New Mexico, where he found a job as a ranch hand.

Because he didn't feel at home in that windy country, Truman gladly accepted an offer from Mr. Whiting to work on his apple farm north of Española in 1932. The young man earned $25 a month, with board. Whiting thought highly enough of him to help him buy six acres and a two-room house next door. That same year, he became the gardener on the estate of painter Randall Davey in Santa Fe.

Truman went back to Arkansas to be married. In 1939 he and his wife moved to their fifteen acres in Fairview, New Mexico, where they established a truck farm. For the next fourteen years, they supplied stores in Santa Fe with their fresh produce. In 1953, Truman became chief gardener at the New Mexico School for the Deaf, while continuing to grow and deliver fresh produce in Santa Fe.

But times were growing ripe for Truman's special contribution to the community from his own knowledge and experience of the land. In 1968, a group of five families got together to sell their fresh vegetables in Los Alamos; the following year, they moved their trucks to a church school parking lot on Agua Fria Street in Santa Fe. With Truman's guiding energy and vision, those first attempts at bringing the fresh produce of northern New Mexico growers directly to the public evolved into what is now one of Santa Fe's most vital and beloved summer rituals—the Santa Fe Area Farmers Market in Sanbusco Center, where dozens of growers congregate with delighted buyers of fruits, vegetables, flowers, wreaths, jams, pestos, and freshly baked goods every Tuesday and Saturday morning.

"If you just grow onions," Truman explained, "people can only buy so many. Some ranchers just take apples to the farmers market. But I grow five kinds of lettuce. You've got to know the varieties, what to plant, and what people want, if you want to make it a success. It's a skill, just like a plumber or a carpenter."

Farming was a year-round occupation for Truman, who carefully timed his crops with the seasons. Starting in late March, he planted something new every week. As a result, he had crops to sell from June throughout the fall. He refused to scrimp on seed; instead, he insisted on starting with the best.

Rejecting many offers to sell his land, he maintained his chosen way of life and continued to farm, living modestly, relying on his ancient tractor, and never missing a day of market.

"I believe it would be hard for someone new to do it," he said. "You've got to grow it, have a market, and know how to sell it. There's a market for good food if you can grow it."

"I've done well because I don't plant just one thing. I grow five kinds of lettuce."

—*Truman Brigham*

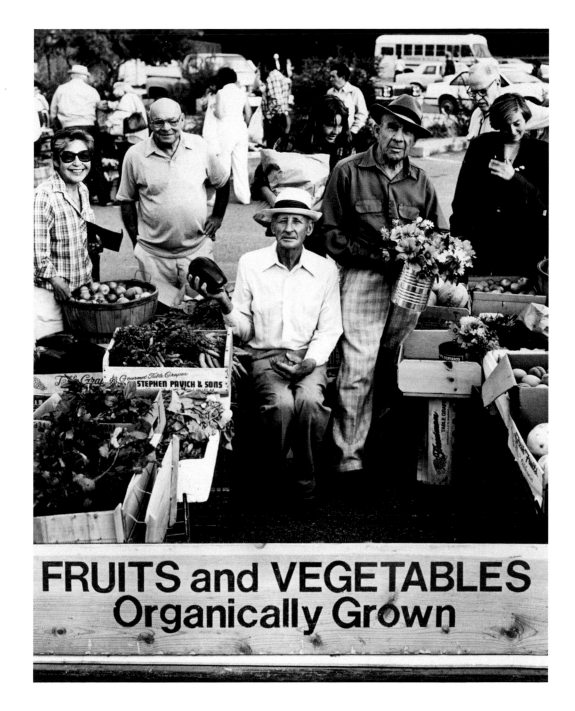

FRUITS and VEGETABLES
Organically Grown

Eleanor Broh-Kahn

NEW MEXICO'S GRANT MAVEN

NEW MEXICO'S ARTISTS call Eleanor Broh-Kahn the "guardian angel of art." As administrative secretary of the Arts Division of the Office of Cultural Affairs, for nearly twenty-five years she handled arts publicity and grants information, and helped artists cope with the frustrations of the grant-writing process. In addition, she was in charge of all publicity and administrative detail for the Governor's Arts Awards program during its first fifteen years.

She was born near Boston in 1924 "into an old New England family with firm *Mayflower* roots." Her father, Edwin, had his own law firm in Boston. Her mother, Beatrice, had a Ph.D. in Semitic languages from Bryn Mawr and taught at Wellesley College. After her father's death in 1929, the family moved to Oxford, Ohio, where her mother was a professor of religion at Western College, at Miami University, also in Oxford, and at other colleges in the Midwest.

Eleanor and her brother, Frank, were raised in a strong academic atmosphere. "I grew up in the library. They had to poke me out with a stick at closing time," she said. After graduating from Miami University with honors in English, Eleanor received the New York Press Association Graduate Fellowship at Syracuse University School of Journalism, where she began work on a master's degree and was an assistant in the Press Association's local office. "I remember not having really clean fingernails for two years because I was getting out press releases on their mimeograph machine," she said. She left to become editor of a house magazine at Bristol Laboratories, the pharmaceutical division of Bristol-Myers, then one of the world's largest penicillin producers. She later became publicity direc-

tor, a post she held until late 1951.

In 1952, Eleanor married Dr. Robert Broh-Kahn, an internist who later founded Bard Pharmaceuticals. She did volunteer work with the Margaret Sanger Research Bureau in New York, working with Dr. Abraham Stone, and served on its board of directors. In the 1960s, the Broh-Kahns lived for two and a half years in Nice, France. When the marriage broke up. Eleanor returned to New York and worked for several years in public relations and editing positions on Madison Avenue.

In 1969, Eleanor came to her mother's home in Santa Fe to recuperate from a broken bone. "Mama had told me that Santa Fe was the most cosmopolitan city in the country. The spell of New Mexico took hold, and I never returned to Manhattan." She worked at the Institute of American Indian Arts on its "Indian Summer" workshop for Native American educators from all over the country. She edited a children's book on Indian music and dance that is still used in intercultural education.

In 1972, Eleanor took a temporary position with the New Mexico Arts Commission to write its annual report to the Legislature. She worked for that same organization, now the Arts Division of the Office of Cultural Affairs, for nearly a quarter century, and retired as of 1997.

Eleanor recalls the creation of the National Endowment for the Arts in 1965. "In those days, you had to be in a big city or on a college campus to see great theater and opera, attend major concerts and dance programs, and have really good exposure to the arts. Any cuts to the endowment, and the Republicans' plan to disband it completely, are truly a step backward, back into the Dark Ages."

"I foresee that Santa Fe will remain the unique artistic community that it is and become a national model for . . . support of the arts of all . . . our cultures."

—*Eleanor Broh-Kahn*

Anthony & Gita Brooke

INTERNATIONAL PEACE NETWORKERS

It's a story out of Kipling, or Jospeh Conrad. In 1841 English adventurer James Brooke helped the Sultan of Brunei pacify rebellious Dayak tribes. The Sultan rewarded Brooke by ceding him the adjoining state of Sarawak. For a hundred years, the Brookes ruled Sarawak, on the island of Borneo, as their private fiefdom, under British protection. Theirs was the only European dynasty in Asia.

In 1946 Anthony Brooke was next in line to rule. He sided with Sarawak nationalists fighting for independence from colonial rule. His uncle, then in power, chose to cede the state to Britain at that time. Anthony was banished from the country. He was allowed to return only seventeen years later, when Sarawak became part of the Federation of Malaysia.

In India Anthony met Gita Keiller, a member of the Swedish royal family. The couple entered into a lifelong partnership as peace activists and campaigners on behalf of indigenous peoples. Unabashed idealists in a cynical time, in 1975 they founded Operation Peace Through Unity, convinced that "The future lies in the hands of the people of the world." Their quarterly newsletter, Many to Many, is a sort of international bulletin board, an anticipation of the World Wide Web, compiling news items, strategies, poems and letters from around the world, for use in the cause of peace, environmental protec-tion and the rights of indigenous peoples.

While the Brookes now reside in New Zealand, where they "rest" between their personal world peace tours, they have in the past lived in Santa Fe. Their work involves gathering together people, ideas, and inspiration on behalf of peace. They are among the rare people who are so moved by their cause that they have taken matters into their own hands, evolving their own means of working as they go. They are motivated, as Anthony says, by "internal fire, enthusiasm, and a positive belief in humanity."

Some of their major focuses have included the establish-ment in Antarctica of a peace park; the World Disarmament Campaign Petition in Western Australia; and the promotion of "new tourism," or eco-tourism, as a way peace can become "good business."

While the Brookes do not solicit money for their causes, they do ask that people become committed to working within their communities by actively "thinking globally and acting locally."

As Anthony says, "Let our enthusiasm and love of all life on our beloved planet render our quest for peace irresistible, irrepressible, and the longed for outcome—unavoidable!"

"We fully trust
the human spirit.
We believe in its
beauty, its
courage. We fully
trust that there is
a plan and a pur-
pose, and every
challenge
humanity is con-
fronted with is
there for a very
good reason."
—*Gita Brooke*

Alice Bullock

A LOVE OF WORDS

I CAN'T REMEMBER WHEN I COULDN'T READ," said well-known Santa Fe author and teacher Alice Bullock. "We didn't have a lot of books because coal camp people didn't have a lot of money." Her mother purchased the complete works of Charles Dickens from a traveling salesman, and "she was so disgusted because I had read them all before the first payment was due," Alice said.

Alice was born in Buck, Oklahoma in 1904. Her father worked as a stationary steam engineer, at the coal mines. When his wife was diagnosed as in danger of developing tuberculosis, he found a job in the high, dry climate of Gardiner, New Mexico, a mining town outside Raton. "We came out in 1912, the year the territory became a state," Alice recalled. "I was born in New Mexico—at the age of eight...In my heart, I'm a New Mexican."

She liked growing up in a coal camp. "We used to hitch up Old Blue, our horse," to go to Raton to buy groceries, a risky undertaking because mine employees were required to purchase their food from the company store. Had they been caught, her father would have lost his job, Alice said. Monday was wash day, and young Alice drew water from a well to do the family's laundry.

Alice attended school in Gardiner through eighth grade and at age eleven began working at the coal company's hospital. During the four years that she attended high school in Raton, she worked as a maid for a different family each year.

Her teaching career began in Elizabethtown in the 1920s, where she taught miners' children. Later she taught in tiny ranching and mining communities—Sofia, Optimo, Van Houten, and Gardiner. She met her husband, Dale Bullock, when he came to interview her for winning a teaching award. "If you were married, you weren't allowed to teach," she recalled. Her husband was the editor of the *Raton Reporter*, and because she couldn't teach after their marriage, Alice became interested in writing for the paper. Alice and Dale raised two daughters, Carlotta and Patricia.

The Bullocks moved to Santa Fe in 1941. Alice worked as secretary to the superintendent of schools. She also bought Corrine's Dress Shop, which she owned for several years, renaming it Bullock's of Santa Fe.

Her career as an author began when Alice was asked to write a history of the Santa Fe schools. For fifteen years, she reviewed books for the *New Mexican*. She could read an "ordinary book in two hours."

Alice discovered that she liked to travel and began collecting stories of small town folk. Her first book was *Living Legends of the Santa Fe Area.* She also wrote *Discover Santa Fe, Mountain Villages of New Mexico, Loretto and the Miraculous Staircase, Squaw Tree,* and *Monumental Ghosts.* In addition, she taught herself photography so that she could take pictures to accompany her writing. Her books, articles, and photographs relate stories of life in the coal camps and northern New Mexico legends.

In later years, Alice lost her eyesight but not her love of the written word. She listened to fifteen talking books each week and was elated when she received the first recorded version of *New Mexico Magazine.*

"If everybody
had to draw
water from a
well . . . there
wouldn't be
any wasted
water."

—Alice Bullock

Jacques Cartier

FIRE DANCER EXTRAORDINAIRE

Jacques Cartier was born on a ship in the Indian Ocean at the turn of the century as his parents were en route to a diplomatic post. His exact age isn't known, friends say, because Jacques gave his age based on what role he was vying for.

Jacques attended military school till age sixteen, and then enrolled at Vanderbilt University. When an elderly Shakespearean actor and his young actress wife visited the campus, Jacques took to the stage as a spear holder for the performances. Before the run concluded, the "beautiful" young actress had kissed Jacques and suggested he consider becoming an actor.

He cabled his father in Johannesburg, South Africa, and requested permission to attend drama school. His father's reply was succinct, "No."

Jacques followed his dreams despite his father's objection. "I had some diamonds that my mother gave me," Jacques said; he sold a few and went to New York City to attend the American Academy of Dramatic Art. Several weeks later, he was "kicked out for having no talent."

Out of diamonds and jobless, he was sleeping on a park bench, and hadn't eaten for four days, when a friend saw him on the street, invited him to dinner, and offered to tell her director that Jacques was a dancer. "She said that he would give me a job, and she would show me what to do," he recalled. The director asked Jacques to audition. "I haven't the vaguest idea what I did," Jacques said, but he was hired.

Flo Ziegfeld saw Jacques perform a Javanese dance and asked him to join the Ziegfeld Follies, where he starred with Fanny Bryce, W. C. Fields, and Eddie Cantor. Wanting to learn more about dance, Jacques went to see Ruth St. Denis. St. Denis had seen him in the Follies and said, "'You don't need a teacher, you need to hire a small hall and work. Put your ideas into dance form.' That's exactly what I did, and that is how I became a dancer," he said.

Movie roles and international acclaim followed. The *New York Times* lauded Jacques as "America's Greatest One-Man Theater" for his portrayals of such figures as the Apache Chief Cochise and the Russian dancer Nijinsky.

Jacques arrived in Santa Fe in the early 1920s. In 1926, his lifelong friend Will Shuster created Zozobra, Old Man Gloom, as part of Fiesta de Santa Fe. Jacques became the Fiesta's beloved fire dancer, performing year after year alongside the gigantic puppet Old Man Gloom, burned to dispel the misfortune and unhappiness of the preceding year. Shuster's first Zozobra was five feet tall, and Jacques easily performed his fire dance. The third Zozobra was thirty-five feet tall. Dwarfed by Old Man Gloom, "I can remember thinking, you're too little to do this," Jacques said. "Zozobra would send up bunches of burning excelsior. Often it would come down on my shoulder. I'd brush it off, but was burned. My wife, Zena, would put a patch on [my costume]—year after year, patches went over patches."

A renowned dancer and performer, Jacques was also a guiding force in the growth of many cultural and humanitarian institutions in Santa Fe. He gained an international reputation in landscape design. One of his Santa Fe gardens earned him a Frank Lloyd Wright award.

"Zozobra would send up bunches of burning excelsior. Often it would come down on my shoulder."   —*Jacques Cartier*

Modesta Charley

PRESERVING CEREMONIAL DRESS

"THESE TEWA DRESSES have a special traditional pattern using tiny tucks and traditional gussets under the arm," Modesta Charley showed us her handiwork. "We usually use a regular white material, forty-five inches wide. You use the edge to make the pleats. Every year I would make one dress, and every year it would win a prize. Now they have a machine to make the gathers—the pleats."

Born the daughter of Santiago and Delorita Martinez at San Juan Pueblo in 1905, Modesta lived with her mother and sister, Raycita. "My father passed away. My mother made pottery for her living," said Modesta. "There was a Spanish lady who used to sew for us. We didn't have a sewing machine, so she made our clothes. . . . My mother paid her with the pottery that she made."

Once or twice a month the family loaded up the wagon and headed to Santa Fe to sell the pottery. "We didn't get all the way to Santa Fe," Modesta recalled. "We got to a place where the water runs across the highway. There were a lot of cotton-wood trees. We would stay there during the night. In the morning, we'd eat breakfast and go on in to Santa Fe. There were just a few stores then."

Modesta attended school in San Juan until fourth grade, when she went to boarding school in Santa Fe. "I never came back to the village," she said. "My mother passed away during the big flu the first year I was in Santa Fe. The field nurse took a liking to me, and she always looked after me. I learned to make fancy lace, and she sold my bobbin lace. That's how I earned money." She then learned to make buttonholes at ten cents apiece.

After eighth grade, Modesta studied business at the Haskell Institute in Lawrence, Kansas, now Indian Nations University. She took Civil Service tests and was assigned to a job at the Indian hospital in Tuba City, Arizona, but didn't report for work immediately. "I came home for the first time," she said.

Tuba City was deserted when Modesta arrived on Halloween night. "Everybody had gone to Luke, Arizona, for a Halloween party. Nobody was there except one old man with grey hair. He met me and took me to a house where I had my room. I sure was crying. I wanted to come home," she said. She held out for two years, then returned to Santa Fe.

While in Tuba City, Modesta met Sam Charley, a Hopi. "He was a cowboy, and he was working for a trading post," she said. "He came looking for me in Santa Fe. He was a good-looking man." They married, and both got jobs at the Santa Fe Indian School. Modesta and Sam raised three children: John, Alfred, and Marie.

Modesta began weaving ceremonial belts after she retired in 1970. She traveled to Sedona, Arizona, "to learn to weave the traditional Hopi patterns. For the belts, we spin the yarn before we do the weaving."

In 1980, Modesta returned to live at the pueblo she'd left as a child. "The governor wrote me and said I could have a house," she remembered the happy day. "I moved in."

"I already knew
how to do general
weaving, but I
wanted to learn
how to do the
belt weave."

—*Modesta Charley*

Manuel "Bob" Chavez

FULFILLING A PROMISE TO THE GREAT SPIRIT

EIGHTEEN HUNDRED MEMBERS of the New Mexico National Guard set out on the Bataan Death March, in April 1942, after US entry into the Second World War. Nine hundred came back alive. Bob Chavez, born and raised in Cochiti pueblo, was one of the survivors. During his four years as a prisoner of war in the Philippines and Japan, he made a promise to the Great Spirit. He vowed that if he made it back to New Mexico, he would devote himself to his school, St Catherine's Indian School, where he was a member of the first graduating class in 1935.

Back in New Mexico at war's end, Bob went to work as an airplane mechanic for Southwest Airlines and for the State Highway Department, in order to support his family, wife Mary, a childhood friend from Cochiti, and their children. And, drawing on his talents as an athlete and an artist, he began to make good on his wartime promise.

First he volunteered as a sports coach at St Catherine's. In 1953, he introduced track into the curriculum and built a winning team. In 1955 he began teaching art classes in a basement studio he and his wife themselves constructed at the school. He volunteered all his free time on evenings and weekends as coach and teacher. He paid for supplies out of his own pocket, or by bartering paintings. Twice a year his students held shows and split the proceeds with the art program, to keep it going.

Bob never understood why his grandmother, from Cochiti, gave him a Hopi name. He didn't know what it meant, till he met a Hopi in Sheridan, Wyoming who told him that Ow-u-Te-wa means Echo of Spring. He wears his poetic name and his artistic reputation modestly. "Everyone says I'm an artist. I've never claimed to be an artist," he insists. His paintings took first prize at Indian Market first time out, in 1933, when he was all of eighteen. After the war, the dedicated teacher put his own artistic career on hold for years. He was in his forties before he returned to painting. Self-taught as an artist, he paints delicate watercolors depicting Pueblo life, its dances and ceremonies.

Bob continues to divide his time between Cochiti Pueblo and Santa Fe. At the pueblo he's an active participant in ceremonial dances. At St Catherine's he coaches basketball and teaches art. Many of his students have gone on to become teachers and artists in their own right.

"Teaching kids is my greatest pleasure," he told us. "I always say to the kids, 'The Great Spirit has been good to me, to have this natural talent.' I won't say that I want to repay— but I do want to do what I can, as long as I can."

Capitol City Title Services, Inc. & LaMerle Boyd

"Someday, when the Great Spirit calls me, am I going to take that talent with me? I want to leave it with someone who can carry on."
—Manuel "Bob" Chavez

Peggy Pond Church

A PASSION FOR POETRY

BEST KNOWN AS THE AUTHOR of the 1959 classic about the Manhattan Project *The House at Otowi Bridge: The Story of Edith Warner and Los Alamos*, Peggy Pond Church had an abiding love for poetry. Her literary life included decades of work as a serious poet. In fact, she was the only New Mexico native to take an active part in the modernist poetry movement that flourished in Santa Fe from the 1920s through the 1930s. Her career included publication of eight volumes of poetry plus the posthumous collection *This Dancing Ground of Sky: The Selected Poetry of Peggy Pond Church.*

Peggy's first book, *Foretaste,* was published in 1933 as one of the original Santa Fe Editions that gave a significant voice to the literary community of the time. While her work appeared in such prestigious venues as the *Atlantic Monthly*, Peggy said, "I never had the self-confidence" to pursue a career as a public poet. Nonetheless, she continued writing and producing poetry throughout her lifetime.

Although her name is inevitably associated with Los Alamos, where her father, Ashley Pond, Jr., ran the Los Alamos Ranch School that was taken over by the Manhattan Project in 1942, Peggy Pond Church's roots are deeply entwined with other regions of New Mexico.

Peggy was born in Watrous, New Mexico, in 1903, where her great-grandfather raised Clydesdale horses. Her great-grandfather arrived on "one of the first trains through Raton," and at one time managed a ranch for the notorious Senator Stephen Dorsey in the northeastern part of the state. The family also ranched in the Roswell area for a time.

Although Peggy was discouraged by her parents from writing poetry, she remained deeply influenced by their readings of *King Lear, Mother Goose*, and the works of Rudyard Kipling. As a young girl, she loved to ride out into Parajito Canyon on her white horse, Sam, and there she found her first poem:

> *Oh bird so blue*
> *Will you tell me true*
> *What makes you so happy today.*

She considered those days of her early discoveries of poetry to be the best time of her life.

Peggy went on to higher education at progressive schools on the East and West coasts after graduating from Santa Fe High School in 1917. After attending Smith College for two years, she left to marry the teacher Fermor S. Church. They lived for a time in Berkeley, California, where they raised three sons, returning to Santa Fe in 1960.

To cultivate her inner voice and vision, she recorded her dreams. In summer 1945, she dreamed of a great windstorm sweeping down the mountains,"an irresistible, invincible force . . . .about to destroy the earth." This prescient dream, lifted "right out of" her journal, figures in *The House at Otowi Bridge*.

Her love of language and nature, and her desire to record and preserve the beauty of both, comprise Peggy's enduring legacy to New Mexico.

"I've always just written for love. I loved sound, and I loved the poetry I read."   —*Peggy Pond Church*

My sky
is blue and clean
I have not had to
live under the fouled sky
of any city.
I have not had to know hunger or persecution
or rape by any man - evil
I have kept myself virgin
except to my dream lovers,
Virgin even in my marriage.
I have never had to go forth
out of my childhood's Eden.

True, I have forgot the image of my mother's
lifelong,
She whom I would not be
but am
" Falada, Falada,
Is it you hang there?

" If your mother only knew
Her heart would surely break in two.

Willard Clark

ENGRAVED IN THE HEART OF SANTA FE

"I'VE BEEN A PAINTER ever since I can remember," said Willard Clark. "The engravings came about because I needed engravings for my print shop. I needed to make some money."

Born in 1910 to Willard and Lena Clark in Somerville, Massachusetts, Willard spent his childhood in Buenos Aires. His father was president of General Motors of Argentina.

When twelve year old Willard was sent from Argentina to boarding school in the US, he began his formal training in art at the Grand Central School in New York City.

Willard was nineteen, and on his way to California in 1928, when he stopped in Santa Fe to visit friends. Willard, who spoke Spanish fluently, fell in love with the people, the culture, and the land, which reminded him of Argentina.

He met Bertha Berchtold at a country club dance and married her in 1930. Together they built a home and established a print shop on Sosoya Lane in 1931. "The house was built by me because I didn't have any money, and it was the only way I knew to get a house," Willard said. "It started out as a place to work, and then I turned it into a place to live." The Clarks raised two daughters, Doris and Bertha.

Willard's expertise as a printer and his congeniality were praised by others. "My print shop was my living," Willard said. There he did "all types of printing," including the Newman typeface Willard used, which has come to be associated with Santa Fe. He printed "thousands of letterheads, envelopes, office forms—everything a printer has to do," he said. "I wanted to use my art to embellish my printing." Willard learned to make woodcuts and engravings so he wouldn't have to wait ten days for zinc etchings to be sent to Denver. "Nobody in those days waited ten days for a print job. You got the job in the afternoon, you delivered the next day. That's the way it was."

Willard went to work in Los Alamos in 1943. "I was a machinist, a tool and die maker. After the war stopped, I was planning on coming home and reopening my print shop, but it seemed to me at the time that the family would be better off if I stayed with what I was doing." He retired from Los Alamos National Laboratory in the mid-1970s.

In 1982, after 40 years "dormant as a printer" Willard took up his craft again. "With my engraving that I've been doing . . . I challenged myself. Recently, I started a little series of wood engravings to see how many lines I could engrave per inch . . . . I reached some 130-odd lines per inch. I can say I probably have done the best engraving of my life."

His craft advanced; his gaze retreated. The forty-six new wood engravings in *Recuerdos de Santa Fe 1928-1943* revisit a quiet, intimate town, long gone by the 1980's. He printed the engravings for the entire limited edition of one hundred copies. Grandson Kevin Ryan is still handprinting the accompanying text. Later he plans to complete his grandfather's last, unfinished book of engravings, tellingly entitled *The Simple Life*.

"All my life I wanted to do the finest engraving I was capable of."

—*Willard Clark*

Mary Lou Cook

A DESIGN FOR LIFE

TEACHER? CALLIGRAPHER? AUTHOR? MINISTER? Craftsperson? Activist? Volunteer? It's not really possible to label Mary Lou Cook, founder of Santa Fe Living Treasures. Having cultivated the philosophy and practice of honoring the creative impulse in herself and others, she has followed that impulse wherever it led, while encouraging others to do likewise.

"Anything that I do with my hands makes me happy," she said. That includes planting trees, designing proclamations as the official calligrapher of the city of Santa Fe, and practicing the simple craft of Pastecraft™, a craft using fabric and paste to cover solid objects, which she developed and now teaches to help people express their creativity. "The feeling of creating something beautiful that never existed before in the world, and creating it from something that was going to be thrown away, is wonderful," Mary Lou said.

Born in Chicago in 1918, Mary Lou, with her family moved to El Paso soon after her birth, in hopes the climate there would heal her father's tuberculosis. The young bank president died at age thirty-nine. Spending a great deal of time with her grandparents in Kansas City, Mary Lou then studied fine arts at Kansas University and the Kansas City Art Institute. After marrying Sam Cook, she and her family, including three children moved to many different areas. In several cities Mary Lou joined the Junior League and launched successful volunteer ventures, such as a preschool for blind children in Kansas City and a children's arts program in Milwaukee. "I trust myself. When I have the feeling I want to do something, I just do it. I don't know how to be any other way," she said.

With Sam's early retirement, he and Mary Lou settled in Santa Fe in 1969. The list of progressive Santa Fe organizations of which she is a member or founder includes: Concerned Citizens for Nuclear Safety, Business for Social Responsibility, the Greer Garson Theatre Guild, Habitat for Humanity, Community Peace Forum, and Santa Fe Network for the Common Good, which designates the Living Treasures. She was founding director of one of the first minority owned national banks in the US, United Southwest Bank.

Diagnosed with chronic leukemia in 1975, Mary Lou has lived with the illness for decades, embracing alternative health care, counseling others with serious illnesses, and following a spiritual path of good works.

The idea of tree planting as a civic ceremony (trees are planted to honor the Living Treasures) arose when Mary Lou and friends planted thirty-six trees in DeVargas Park to honor Sam Cook the year after his death.

In 1988, on her seventieth birthday, Mary Lou was herself designated a Living Treasure.

"The door opens, someone comes in and it's the right person. I'm understanding this process, of trusting the universe."

Nancy Dahl, Jane Shea, James Borders, Jack & Lou Ryan

"The creative
urge is strongest
in all of us. If
we don't have a
creative outlet,
we're not
healthy and
whole."

—*Mary Lou Cook*

Helen Cordero

STORYTELLER CREATOR

When Cochiti Pueblo potter Helen Cordero reached her forties, she found herself dissatisfied with her work. She couldn't understand why her "pots never turned out too good." At a relative's suggestion, she began making clay figures instead of the traditional pots. Those early figures of the 1960s evolved into the now-familiar storyteller doll, the grandfather figure, who, with open mouth, sits with his grandchildren perched on him as they listen to his stories.

The storyteller is Helen's representation of her grandfather. "He was a very old man," she remembered. "He used to tell us all stories, and he'd put us on his lap or wherever we could sit. He was a great storyteller."

Born in 1915, Helen lived all her life at Cochiti Pueblo, adhering to her traditional way of life heedless of the fame and fortune that came her way. She continued to dig her own white clay, to prepare her natural red and black pigments, and to work outdoors in warm weather and at her kitchen table in the winter. Her husband and son drove one hundred miles to bring home the cedar wood she used to fire her pieces, covered with cow manure, on an open iron grate behind her house.

It was partially the encouragement she received early on from collector Alexander Girard, who bought her first figures, that enabled her to continue on her path, a path that led to the revival of figurative pottery, a tradition that dates back to pre-historic Pueblo cultures. This tradition ceased with the arrival of the Spanish, since figurative pottery was condemned as idolatrous.

"She really caused a revolution or renaissance in Pueblo ceramics. Her genius was that she took an exiting tradition, did something different with it, and it simply caught on. As a result the whole shape of Pueblo pottery has changed," says Barbara Babcock, author of *The Pueblo Storyteller*, a book about Helen.[*]

"It's a very, very unique phenomenon in Pueblo ceramics for someone to just turn a new corner," said Stephen Becker, director of the Museum of Indian Arts and Culture in Santa Fe.[**]

During her lifetime, Helen saw her works, which she once sold for under $10, command high prices. Hundreds of Helen's works are now housed in the Girard Wing of the Museum of International Folk Art in Santa Fe, as well as at the Smithsonian Institution, the Heard Museum in Phoenix, and many other museums around the country.

Although she went her own way as a potter—in a style now widely imitated—Helen always held to traditional Pueblo beliefs about the spiritual nature of her work. "She [the clay, the earth] is very close to me. I am with her, and she knows it, and she helps me create my grandfather. It seems like she tells me, and I do as she tells me" [***]

---

[*]   Hollis Walker, "She Still Lives Within the Clay," *New Mexican*, n.d.
[**] Hollis Walker, "Creator of Storyteller Dolls Dies," *New Mexican*, n.d.
[***] Hattie Clark, "A Storyteller in Clay," *Christian Science Monitor*, November 2, 1987.

"All my potteries come out of my heart. They're my little people. I talk to them and they're singing. If you're listening, you can hear them."**

—Helen Cordero

Cordelia Coronado

WEAVER OF TRADITION

CORDELIA CORONADO'S LIFE IS ROOTED IN TRADITION and the land. All her activities, including her personal life, her community service, and her art, harmoniously function to preserve the way of life she loves. Mother of eight, Medanales postmaster for thirty years, teacher, gardener extraordinaire, choir leader, and water rights activist, Cordelia is above all known for her fine Rio Grande Valley weaving.

"I am very content here, doing what I am doing. I'm happy with what I am, and I love it. I have no ambitions to amass physical possessions or money. As long as I have a good roof over my head and food on my table, that's all I need," she says.

Cordelia traces her weaving lineage to her paternal grandfather, Isidore Martinez, whose work influenced the Chimayó weaving houses. At ninety-six, her mother was still weaving and selling her famous rag rugs. Born in Medanales in 1933, Cordelia eventually left for California but returned in 1957 to take over as postmaster when her father retired. Working in the afternoons left her plenty of time for weaving during the mornings "when the winters were long." She taught weaving from her studio and at Ghost Ranch as well. "Weaving is very therapeutic," she says. "On a bad day, it melts troubles away."

While each blanket she weaves is unique in color combination and design, Cordelia is quick to acknowledge her weaving ancestry. "My ancestors on both sides were Navajo. When the Spanish brought sheep and wool, they started weaving Indian patterns. There's no clear picture of: is it Spanish? Is it Indian? It's like the people—we're part Indian, we're part Spanish, we're part Anglo."

For all her love of weaving and the recognition she has achieved for her art, her "garden is the main thing. Weaving is just a hobby." She not only grows food for her family but sells corn, peppers, and dahlia bulbs—the flower and vegetable strains she has developed over the years. "Gardening is my life," she says. "Just to see the little plants emerge from nothing—it's like a child. If you tend it with care and love, it will respond."

As treasurer of the Rio de Chama Acequias Association, Cordelia works to preserve the water and farming rights of the families in her community. *"Si no hay agua, no hay vida,"* she says. "If there's no water, there's no life."

Living in a community makes self-sufficiency possible. "Sure, we can go to work in Santa Fe. But why our area is special is that it's more comforting, more fulfilling to do it here with our neighbors."

Within her own family, Cordelia has carpenters, electricians, concrete workers—all the necessary tradespeople to build a home within a month. "It's why, without monetary resources, we all have our own homes. Not elegant, but livable. Community must be built within a family. The worries are far and few because we all pull together. When somebody needs a well, we all pitch in."

She sums up her philosophy of life. "If you take every hour of the day at a time, it will take care of itself. I live each day as if it were the last, treat everybody the best I know how, and I work hard, play hard, and fight hard."

"You don't have time to think about the bad things when you are concentrating on weaving."

—*Cordelia Coronado*

Ann Dasburg

ALWAYS WORKING FOR PEACE

"It was in the 1980s that I became involved in the Environmental Movement," said Ann Dasburg. "At the same time, I became acquainted with the writings and teachings of Thich Nhat Hahn. His teachings about peace and the interrelationship of all sentient beings led me to follow a Buddhist path."

She was born at home to Maude and Ward Jackson in 1916 in Cleveland Heights, Ohio. Ann's father owned a lumber company. She grew up with two sisters, Elizabeth and Mary.

Ann was thirteen when her father died, "the day before the great stock market crash," she said. "My mother's parents lost everything. We sold the house, and they moved in with us. I realized I would have to prepare to earn my own living."

Ann attended the Laurel School in Cleveland through high school. "I went on to college to be a teacher, but the real basis of my education was at Laurel," Ann said. "I received an excellent education."

She met and married medical student Andy Kerr in 1940. While Andy served in Europe during World War II, Ann "started a nursery school in Rochester for all the women who were working in the war effort," she said. "The training I got from my involvement with the Rochester Junior League set the pace for all the volunteer work I've done in my life, but I quit when the league wouldn't allow a black friend to join." She also started an integrated day care center "to promote good race relations within the community."

She married Al Dasburg, an electrical engineer and son of Taos painter Andrew Dasburg, in 1963. That year she "fell in love with Al and New Mexico."

When Al graduated from MIT, back in 1932, his father bought him 80 acres of the Barberia Ranch, ten miles south of Santa Fe. The sale price was $200. The Barberia Ranch was a familiar, welcome sight for travelers on the Santa Fe Trail. It took its name from a barber on the premises, whose patrons stopped for a shave before heading into town to woo the local women. In 1974 Al and Ann came to live in Santa Fe year round. Bill Lumpkins, the architect, designed his second solar house for them, on their Barberia spread. "The greatest thing that happened in my life was to come out here and realize that this was where I was supposed to be," Anne affirms.

As an activist, she is quick to spot a need and quick to fill it. For an antidote to macho debate in the Gulf War, she founded a new peace group, The Gathering of Women, recruiting members through an ad in the paper. With People for Peace, she encourages the planting of "peace poles" in schools and playgrounds.

Her frequent letters to the editor, from a "different perspective," improve the public debate on community issues. She's published dozens and composed dozens more in her head, on the two mile dirt road beween her house and the highway. Another sign, perhaps, that she's where she's supposed to be—like so many New Mexicans, she does her serious thinking out of doors.

Mary, Katherine, Jay, Jeremy, Reed, Andy, Eowyn, Ward, Avery, Eleanore, Shirley, Nick, Annette, Logan & Susan

"I've always
been involved
with peace work.
I can't think of a
time when I
wasn't."

—*Ann Dasburg*

Mary Woodard Davis

TEXTILE ARTIST

Born in Dewey, Oklahoma, in 1901, when the region was still Indian territory, Mary Woodard Davis enjoyed a multifaceted career that took her to Broadway and Europe before bringing her to Santa Fe. Whether designing sets with Cecil Beaton for *My Fair Lady*, teaching Turkish women to quilt, or creating commissioned pieces of her own textile art at age eighty-seven, she had no qualms about following her own direction wherever it led. "[I've] always been my own person," she said. "I've never been in one niche in life."

Mary's charmed path led her to careers in the New York theater as an actress, director, producer, costume and set designer, and theater owner; she also became a university professor and textile artist. During her career Mary worked with people as diverse as Marlene Dietrich and Turkish women living behind the veil.

One of seven children, Mary learned her sustaining craft of needlework early in life. Her father, an attorney and legal expert in Indian land titles, was also a strong believer in education. He sent Mary to convent school in Kansas City, Missouri, where she learned fine needlework, drawing and painting, the springboard for her later artistic success. Other individuals who influenced this future master quilt artist were an aunt, who taught Mary to do a five-patch by the time she was five years old, and the Ozark quilters she met in Arkansas early in the century.

Following two years at the University of Oklahoma, Mary taught briefly, then married. In 1931, she returned to school and earned her degree. Eventually, she received an M.A. from Carnegie Tech and later taught at Fordham University.

During a life that involved worldwide travel to countries such as England, Greece, and Turkey, her career as a university professor served as an anchor in various communities. Although she married twice and raised a son, she persisted in focusing on her work. "A husband of mine was always in the background," is how she put it.

Mary taught thousands of people to quilt during her twenty-five years of teaching. Following her "retirement" to Santa Fe in 1960, she organized a textile workshop in connection with the Museum of International Folk Art. There, in the course of fifteen years, she taught over three thousand students quilt making, weaving, stitchery, and design.

"I'm a real traditionalist in most everything but design," she said. "You can tell I'm not just somebody who decided to make a quilt. I know what has to go into a quilt."

Mary became captivated with the quilt as an art form decades before its current popularity. Her own quilts became recognizable for their bold contemporary designs featuring traditional elements. She was guided by the satisfaction that came from the communal aspect of quilting and from being a consummate craftsperson. "I love the people getting together," she said, "and, of course, that's what kept quilting alive. It's a neighborly thing. Quilting is difficult, it's tedious, it's time-consuming. "But it's satisfying, and you have great pride in what you do if it's done well. I enjoy 'em all the time I'm doin' 'em. I've enjoyed life as it came along. I have a message for all women to enjoy themselves and be happy. Do what you'd like to do, as often as you can."

"Being happy is something you do for yourself. No one else does it for you."

—*Mary Woodward Davis*

Stan & Zu Davis

TOWN AND COMMUNITY BUILDERS

S TAN DAVIS, THE FOUNDER of Davis & Associates, General Contractors, is known for the many buildings he constructed in Santa Fe and northern New Mexico, as well as his work on the reconstruction of many historic places. And both he and his wife, Zulema (Zu), are known for their civic generosity and volunteer work on behalf of the community.

Meeting the architect John Gaw Meem when he was only fourteen years old no doubt influenced Stan's future direction. His profession eventually led him to collaborate with Meem on significant projects, such as the 1974 restoration of the Santa Fe Plaza. Born in Colorado Springs, Colorado, in 1923, Stan moved to Gallup with his family in 1937. After graduating from the University of New Mexico he became a registered engineer. In 1946, he went to Guam to help rebuild the islands after World War II. He worked on the construction of the naval base. Then, in 1948 he moved to Santa Fe and the following year married Zu, a "local girl." Santa Fe is where Stan and Zu made their home and raised their children.

When a car smashed the portal of the Palace of the Governors, Davis & Associates made the repairs. Stan also refurbished the historic Plaza Hotel in Las Vegas, built the Benedictine Monastery in Pecos, and while helping construct the Christ in the Desert Monastery in Abiquiu met Thomas Merton. By extending financing to the Children's Museum and St. Elizabeth's Shelter, he assisted several of the city's nonprofit and service organizations in obtaining their buildings. All in all, Stan has constructed more buildings in Santa Fe than any other contractor; in addition, he built much of the Air Force Academy in Colorado Springs as well as postwar housing in Los Alamos.

A descendant of the Cabeza de Baca family, Zu attended Loretto Academy when it was a girls' boarding school. She has fond memories of horseback riding up to Hyde Park on Cerro Gordo Road and stopping at the little neighborhood store for a Coke and a candy bar. "Everybody knew you; you knew everybody," is how she described the Santa Fe of her girlhood. "The crazy things they'd pull during Fiesta! It was much more relaxed in those days. You got to know famous people who were down to earth," she recalled.

Zu has taught religion at her church, St. John the Baptist, and been involved in St. Vincent Hospital Auxiliary and many other groups.

Stan has served on the boards of the First Interstate Bank, the College of Santa Fe, and St. Vincent Hospital, and worked with the Boy Scouts of America. Among his many honors is the B'nai Brith Anti-Defamation League's Brotherhood Award, which he received in 1989.

"I think Stan has built or restored most of the important buildings in Santa Fe, including the Palace of the Governors."

—*Zu Davis*

Carol Decker

PROMOTING RESPECT FOR CULTURAL DIFFERENCES

"IN ALL OF THE EXPERIENCES I'VE HAD, I've seen over and over again that unless you can talk with people about the fundamentals of life—of spirit, image, connectedness to the universe—then you are just tinkering," said Carol Decker.

Describing herself as "an old New England Yankee," Carol was the oldest of three children born to Scott and Alma Paradise in 1927. Her father taught English at Phillips Academy in Andover, Massachusetts. "I was a sickly, asthmatic little kid who found solace in books, particularly about the West, where dreams of health and adventure expanded the walls of the bedroom," she recalled.

She started studying Spanish at Abbot Academy. A summer with the Experiment in International Living, spent with a family in Mexico, prompted a major in Spanish and anthropology at Connecticut College. "I went on to work on my master's in Spanish at Columbia, but my real education came from the New York International House, where I lived with people from all over the world," she said. Afterwards, she spent a year in Mexico City's Xochimilco neighborhood with a Quaker community development project.

Carol met her husband, Fred, when both were teaching at a prep school in Arizona. They got married in 1956, and lived in New York and Spain before settling in Connecticut, where Fred taught for the University of Connecticut for eighteen years. They raised a son, Scott, and a daughter, Anne.

Throughout the 1960s, Carol watched the racial/cultural turmoil of the era with growing dismay. "The deaths of Martin Luther King and Bobby Kennedy propelled me into action," she said. "I found myself involved in cross-cultural relations among inner-city blacks, outer-city whites, and immigrant Hispanic groups, developing various innovative projects. Some of these were church-sponsored, which led to deepening interest in the relationships between faith and society—which led to Yale Divinity School."

"I was a gray-head when I graduated with a Master of Divinity in 1977," she recalled. "I then worked as a campus minister at the University of Bridgeport for three years."

The Deckers moved to Santa Fe in 1980. Without a formal ministry, Carol worked with the Ministerial Alliance, helping organize the first Hunger Walks (ecumenical, church-sponsored efforts to raise funds to alleviate world hunger). She worked with Casa de Paz Homeless Shelter and helped develop the Interfaith Council. She also spent several seasons as a tour guide for Grayline Tours and taught conversational Spanish for ten years at Santa Fe Community College.

Out of all these experiences emerged the organization Vecinos del Norte (Neighbors of the North). "I was aware on many levels of the dynamics of the Anglo/Hispanic/Indian connections of this area and was thinking, isn't there something we can do to help people understand each other?" said Carol. "Vecinos celebrates our respective heritages, encourages people to respect other cultures, and looks for ways we can work toward common goals. We know that communications among the cultures are very complex; that trust and friendship develop slowly; and that cross-cultural relationships can be rich, rewarding, and essential to our common future."

"My emphasis has been to build relationships among diverse people."   —*Carol Decker*

Rae Douglas

NORTHERN NEW MEXICO'S CHRISTMAS LADY

RAE DOUGLAS HAS DRIVEN THE ROADS of northern New Mexico for thirty-four years, distributing food, clothing, and household goods to the needy. Her "family" lives in an area "all the way from Santa Fe up to the Colorado line."

"When I first started doing charity work, I could see that poor people didn't have Thanksgiving. They didn't have Christmas. It was just another day to them," said Rae. The "Christmas Lady" had found her calling. Rae loaded up her car and "went to each house [herself] giving out dozens of turkeys, chickens—anything [she] could find—pies, cakes, all the goodies."

She was born Lovina Rae Jackson in 1914 in Plainview, Texas. Her grandparents, Emma and Phillip Jackson, raised her and taught her to care about others, said Rae. "They taught me a long time ago when I was a little tiny girl that whenever anybody comes to you hungry—even if you don't have but one slice of bread—you divide." They also taught her how to work. "When I was five, my grandpa put a milk bucket in my hand and said, 'Let's go to the cow lot.' He gave me a cow of my own, and I learned how to milk."

She attended school in a "little two-room, red brick schoolhouse five miles east of Plainview. My grandparents kept the two teachers as boarders, so they also taught me at night," Rae said. She went to high school in Plainview "but just got through three months of the tenth grade" when she had to quit because her health broke down. Then she "worked on the farm." At nineteen Rae was married briefly and had a son, Robert.

"I was on my way to a rodeo and was putting water in my Model A when I met Winston 'Doug' Douglas. I had the hose in my hand and accidentally squirted water in his brand-new pair of shoes," Rae recalled. A few days later he looked her up in Plainview.

She married Doug, who adopted Robert, in Santa Fe. They moved to Los Alamos in "the last part of 1943 with two dump trucks," said Rae. "We hauled bricks to the State Penitentiary for two years."

While selling home products door-to-door "in the boondocks, I saw poverty," she said. Rae can't begin to estimate how many families she has helped, but a committee of Los Alamos volunteers makes the necessary arrangements so that the Christmas Lady's needy families are adopted for Christmas. Northern New Mexico families provide food for Christmas dinner and gifts for each member of the families they adopt.

Throughout the year, "My community sees to it that I have everything I need—food, clothing, and their generous donations," she said. The second van donated by the town has "got almost 100,000 miles on it," said Rae, who sometimes makes five trips to Chama in a week. "I'm on call twenty-four hours a day. If somebody needs me at 2 A.M., I go. I really don't think that I would have lived to be this age if I hadn't had this . . . work to do."

In 1994, the United Methodist Church of Los Alamos hosted Rae's eightieth birthday celebration. "There was cake and ice cream for the whole congregation, and the choir sang a special song for the occasion, 'I Ain't Got Time to Die.'" She agreed with the sentiment. "I'm going to keep on going. If they lift the lid down, then I'll have to quit."

"Very seldom do I miss a day when I haven't taken care of someone."

—*Rae Douglas*

Dorathea Dunakin

WATCHING SANTA FE EVOLVE

⌀

DOROTHY DUNAKIN ARRIVED in Santa Fe in 1912. She came, with her mother and brother, to join her father. "We came on the Santa Fe (Railway) to Lamy," she recalled. "Then we came on from Lamy, which was the only way to get to Santa Fe, unless you came by horse and buggy."

She was born in Pueblo, Colorado in 1900. Dorothea's father, Adolph Koch, worked for American Laundry Machinery. He had traveled to Santa Fe to install equipment for a laundry owned by La Fonda Hotel. Back then, "Men wore these thick collars, and to get them done up, you had to mail them to Albuquerque," Dorathea said. "At that time, the D&R Chief came by on what is now Guadalupe Street, and . . . that made it very easy to get heavy machinery shipped down." When the hotel decided not to keep the laundry, Adolph purchased it, kept it for a short time, and then opened the Santa Fe Electric Laundry. Located at the corner of Washington and Guadalupe streets, it was so named because electrical equipment was used to run the washing machines.

In 1915, Dorathea's father bought a house on Agua Fria, now 229 Polaco Street. "An irrigation ditch ran down Agua Fria at that time, and the house was surrounded by alfalfa fields," said Dorathea. "The house was originally two stories. It was built before the Civil War," but the top story had burned before the Koch family bought the property. Some of the timbers were stamped "not made by slave labor," and some of the floors were laid with "battleship" linoleum.

"Archbishop Lamy sent for all these trees to give to the churches. He planted all these Carolina poplars" along the ditch on Agua Fria, Dorathea said. "The last one of the Carolina poplars had to be cut down in 1986. Because we watered after the ditch was gone, we had the trees longer than anyone else. I'm sure it was the last tree left in Santa Fe planted by Archbishop Lamy."

Dorathea worked for her father at the laundry after school and on weekends. After high school she went to Chicago for a short time to become a teacher but decided to study nursing instead. "My father didn't like it that I went into nurse's training. He was German, and a daughter's place was at home, helping the mother," she told us. "He told me I had to come home and drive my mother's car. . . . I came home and taught mother to drive her car and then went back to take my nurse's training."

Having earned her cap at St. Luke's in Denver, Dorathea returned home. "No nursing," her father said, but the doctors would call him to ask if Dorathea could come to work. Consequently, she worked as a private duty nurse.

Dorathea married Ray Dunakin on November 7, 1937, and their daughter, Dorathea, was born in 1939. The marriage was brief, and when her father died in 1939, Dorathea lived with her mother, who died at the age of 106.

In Santa Fe, Dorathea is widely respected for her generous volunteer work for the Episcopal Church and Open Hands. Knowing how much her mother valued companionship in her later years, Dorathea volunteered at Open Hands, founded in 1977 to serve Santa Fe County's elder citizens and provide essential services to improve their quality of life.

"I've seen a great many changes in Santa Fe. There were two cars in Santa Fe when we came in 1912."

—*Dorathea Dunakin*

Bertha Dutton

DAUGHTER OF THE DESERT

IT WAS AN AUTOMOBILE ACCIDENT that sent Bertha Dutton on her way toward becoming one of the West's most noted anthropologists. As she stepped off a streetcar in Lincoln, Nebraska, in 1930, a drunk driver hit her. Following her recuperation, she took the insurance money, bought a Model A Ford, and in 1932 headed off to study archaeology at the University of New Mexico in Albuquerque with Dr. Edgar Lee Hewett.

In the course of a distinguished career, Bertha served for twenty five years (1936-61) as curator of ethnology at the University of New Mexico and for ten years as Director of the Museum of Navajo Ceremonial Art (now the Wheelwright Museum). She travelled throughout the hemisphere. She published books and articles. She excavated a house ruin at Chaco Canyon with Hewett and worked extensively at sites in the Galisteo Basin. "I dug, dug,dug," is her modest summation.

Born on an Iowa farm in 1903, she spent fifteen years as a businesswoman before beginning her studies in anthropology. "Bert," as she was known, received her B.A. and M.A. degrees from the University of New Mexico; in 1952, she earned her Ph.D. from Columbia University.

In 1938, after serving as assistant director to Hewett at the Museum of New Mexico, Bertha took over the old armory building in Santa Fe, where she built the ethnology department. There she made furniture and display cases, and designed and catalogued the collection. She invited local Pueblo people to help her create this showplace.

Bertha's circle of friends extended to Indians, who shared their knowledge with her. She was proud of these friendships. "I knew Indians," she said. "I had my friends in all the pueblos. I wouldn't want to live anywhere else in the world. It's just been open doors, if you want to go in."

She also knew Mary Cabot Wheelwright and Georgia O'Keeffe. While driving the artist home to Abiquiu one day, Pedernal, a location of many of Bertha's digs, came into view. "Oh look," she said. "There's my peak." O'Keeffe gave her an icy look and said, "I beg your pardon. I thought that was my peak!"

Bertha began operating the Archaeological Mobile Camps for Senior Girl Scouts in 1947, taking groups of scouts from all over the United States on two-week camping tours of archaeological sites in the Four Corners and Galisteo areas. For years the scouts returned, bringing their children and grandchildren with them.

As a sign of her independence, when she turned twenty-one Bertha cut her long hair. "I was free then," she said, "and I've been free ever since." Instead of attending her college commencement, she took a boat trip to archaeological sites in Peru and Bolivia. "I'm so glad I lived when I did," she said, "without fences and boundaries everywhere."

"I've always
been learning
from the Indians,
past and present.
We're all one
people, you
know."

—*Bertha Dutton*

Betty Egan

MADRE OF RANCHO ENCANTADO

⚭

BETTY EGAN LEFT COLLEGE TO JOIN THE ARMY, headed west to start a dude ranch, and organized a volunteer fire department. *Can't* and *shouldn't* were two words Betty didn't indulge.

Elisabeth Tinnerman Egan was born in 1919, on Guadalupe Day, December 12. "Once she came to New Mexico, she liked to observe the day," said her daughter, Veronica Egan. "She liked the fact that she and Our Lady of Guadalupe shared a day." The daughter of Cleveland industrialist Albert Tinnerman, Betty grew up a tomboy, who loved to fish, hunt, and camp with her father.

She graduated from Dennison College but "ran away from college to join the Women's Army Corps during World War II," Veronica said. While at Fort Knox, Betty met Robert Egan, who was also in the army. They were married at Fort Knox in a military ceremony, but "to satisfy the relatives," a lavish traditional ceremony was later held in Cleveland, Veronica said.

Both husband and wife were shipped to Europe. Stationed in France, Betty was to be promoted to major when she became pregnant. "She was a captain in the most highly decorated WAC unit in the European Theater," said Veronica. "She received the Member of the British Empire medal, which was presented to her by King George." She was shipped stateside in the summer of 1945, returning to Cleveland, where she spent the next eighteen years raising children and involving herself in civic causes.

Betty had always wanted to go west. When Robert died from peritonitis at age forty-six, she rented a Dodge motor home, loaded up her four kids, and spent the summer touring "Colorado, Arizona, Texas, New Mexico, a little bit of Utah,"

Veronica remembers. "But we kept ending up back in Santa Fe. Mom just loved it, and so did I."

Betty moved to Tesuque in 1966. She had only been in the area a couple of weeks when Slim Green, a wrangler from Bishop's Lodge "told her about this run-down dude ranch called Rancho del Monte," Veronica said. "She bought it."

The renovated inn, renamed Rancho Encantado, opened in 1968. Betty "was endeavoring to run a really elegant but relaxed inn, never having done anything like that before," her daughter said. "She was a gifted hostess but not a business person." After watching Betty load the groceries for the ranch into her station wagon, "finally Mr. Kaune took her aside and said, 'You know, Mrs. Egan, you're running a restaurant out there. We could deliver.'"

Rancho Encantado's ambiance, seclusion, and intimacy appealed to celebrities, and Betty's guests included Maria Callas, John Wayne, Henry Fonda, and Jimmy Stewart. The Egan family sold Rancho Encantado in 1995.

"The list of things she did for both individuals and the community as a whole are endless," Veronica said, from hosting numerous benefits to providing lodging when the gas was shut off to Betty's Tesuque neighbors during a fierce winter storm in 1971. "They moved into the ranch until they could heat their homes again. I've spoken with people who moved in, and they said it was like a giant party."

Betty was also instrumental in organizing the Tesuque Volunteer Fire Department, becoming the nation's first woman fire chief.

"She led a volunteer and country club existence in Cleveland, which she detested. She wanted to do something on her own—to go out West."
—Veronica Egan

Photo by Carolyn Wright

Richard & Jean Erdoes

COLLABORATORS FOR ART AND JUSTICE

W HEN THE POLITICAL FERMENT of the 1960s and 1970s brought embattled leaders of the American Indian Movement to Richard Erdoes' door, he took them right in. A refugee from Hitler Europe, he remembered the anti-Nazi movement. "We didnt run out on each other then and we won't run out on you," he told Lakota leaders he had met on photo assignment for Life magazine in South Dakota. He and his wife Jean turned their New York apartment into "a free restaurant, hotel and communications center," for the native American activists.

Refugees learn to improvise. Richard had that knack. Born in Frankfurt in 1912 in a family of opera singers, pianists and composers, he studied at the Berlin Academy, contributing cartoons to anti-Nazi publications. When Hitler siezed Austria in 1938, Richard escaped by skiing across the border into Switzerland.

He arrived in New York with only five dollars. In time he won assignments with Life magazine. He met his wife Jean at Life in 1945. She was an art director at Life, also a typographer and calligrapher who had given her name to a typeface, Jean Morton. They married in 1950. Jean took Richard travelling out west, and to New Mexico in 1952. She lured him with a promise, "I must show you Acoma." In 1972, they moved to Santa Fe.

In his fifties Richard improvised again. He and Jean were living in the hubbub created by their Lakota friends. "Cooking was a big part of it," Jean recalled. "Whole families would show up with kids. We got to know some of the old folks." Richard found jobs at ad agencies for many of these friends and a new career for himself.

The instigator was Lame Deer, a Lakota medicine man who arrived with his possession in a shoebox and stayed two months. "His medicine told him," he insisted, that Richard would write his story. "Impossible," Richard said."Not only am I not a writer, but English is my second language." The medicine man persisted and in the end Richard wrote a sample chapter and an outline"just to get rid of him." Within forty-eight hours, they had a book contract. *Lame Deer, Seeker of Visions*, became a classic, translated into many languages. And Richard, the photographer and illustrator, became a much published author as well, with twenty-five titles to his credit.

He wrote *Lakota Woman* with Mary Crow Dog. The contracted publisher turned it down. It lay in a drawer for ten years. Now it's a classic, known world wide, in book and movie versions.

"I'm the same foolish person I was at twenty,"Richard mused. "My mind is not changed. I'm better now than I ever was. The only sad fact about old age is the moment I have found out where I'm good and what silly things I should no longer do, mainly things for commercial reasons, the time is short to do them."

"I speak Sioux
with a Viennese
accent."
—*Richard Erdoes*

Viola Fisher

ANGEL OF CERRO GORDO PARK

THINK GLOBALLY, ACT LOCALLY is sound advice. The reverse is valid too; it's just more difficult to manage. Viola Fisher has done it all. As a UN public health nutritionist she combatted hunger across the globe. In Santa Fe, she's done great things for her Cerro Gordo neighborhood.

She grew up on a farm outside Post Falls, Idaho. When her parents bought the place, "the cash crop was Delicious apples. Later my father raised sweet Spanish onions..My mother had a route where she would sell fruits, vegetables and eggs."

She attended a "little country two-room grade school a half mile from the house. High school was in Post Falls—three and a half miles if you followed the railroad tracks—if we walked, it was four." At the University of Idaho in Moscow she majored in dietetics.

Work as a hospital dietician left her dissatisifed. "So often, you see a patient, and then they leave. I became very interested in how you prevent illness. I decided to go into public health." The war intervened. She served at military bases in several states, then earned a master's in public health nutrition at Columbia University.

In 1955 she went to Shiraz, Iran to "set up the dietary department" in a brand new hospital. The Shah and Queen Soraya attended opening ceremonies.

Blindness caused by severe vitamin A deficiency, and kwashiorkor— children's failure to thrive due to lack of proteins—were the conditions Viola discovered in east Africa in the early 1960s. The only non-African on a UN/ FAO team, she raised the alarm with key government officials from Nigeria, Ghana, Tanzania and Sierra Leone. The Tanzanians offered her a job, but by then she was committed to a survey of food consumption in India's villages, phase one of an FAO/UNICEF effort to rescue children from malnutrition and hunger.

Working in New Mexico in 1949, Viola "had fallen in love with Santa Fe." She came to stay in 1965. She worked for State Department of Health and retired from the Indian Health Service in 1982.

Cerro Gordo Park is a short walk from her back gate. Through the years, the Santa Fe Canyon Association fought City Hall to keep it a natural park, without baseball or soccer fields. Viola, who has lived near the park, on and off, for almost half a century, set out to convince City Hall that the park was well used as it stood.

"The goatsheads were so thick the kids couldn't play in the tot lot," she recalled. Burrs and cheat grass had to be removed. Trees were planted, and for many years Viola strung together a number of hoses and watered them from her house, as there was no closer source. A Plant Day was held, and native plants took root in the park.

Today, "Cerro Gordo is well used," the Angel of Cerro Gordo Park told us. "It's fun in the spring because kids like to fly their kites. People have birthday parties, and there was even a wedding in the park. The people who love it, love it because it's natural."

"Cerro Gordo Park wasn't used because it was such a mess. Now the park is used. I would like to see . . . more native plants [introduced] so that people can come and see what can grow without a lot of care and water."   —*Viola Fisher*

Murray Friedman

PIONEER OF PAIN CONTROL

KNOWN TO HIS COLLEAGUES AS "DR. MESMER," radiologist Murray Friedman brought blessed relief to his patients through his pioneering work in pain control using hypnotherapy. Alhough he began by utilizing hypnotherapy with cancer patients, he then extended its use to treat people with smoking, obstetrical, and other problems. "I'm often the court of last resort," he said.

Born in 1904 in the railroad town of Altoona, Pennsylvania, Murray became a railroad laborer while still in high school, making thirty-five cents an hour. Altoona, he recalled, "was not a very pleasant town. The only way to get out of there was to work for the railroad and take a train out." Murray became interested in pursuing a medical career early on. The eldest of eight children, whose father was a tailor, Murray delivered his youngest brother at age thirteen. "We didn't have a doctor," he said. "My mother went into labor. She told me what to do, and I did it."

While only a freshman in high school, Murray applied to the University of Pennsylvania, the school where he eventually obtained his degrees. Meanwhile, he became impressed by the family doctor, a homeopath. "He made me curious about medicine. And my mother encouraged me. She was a remarkable woman, and she wanted me to go as far as I could."

At the University of Pennsylvania Murray got scholarships and washed dishes at frat houses to put himself through undergraduate and medical school. "I didn't do much else, except study and wash dishes."

Murray became interested in radiology, he said, because it "represented as near an exact science as I could reach in medicine." He picked the best place to become a resident, Columbia University, but when he arrived, no residencies were available. Nevertheless, he asked to be allowed to simply observe, which he did for six months, until he was offered a residency.

Later on, in the midst of his practice, while providing radiation therapy, Murray found many of his cancer patients becoming dependent on drugs. In hopes of finding an alternative to drugs, he became adept at hypnotherapy. It was not a widely understood or accepted treatment at the time, but his patients responded positively. "When I retired from radiology, my patients followed me."

Murray moved to Santa Fe in 1943 and was "immediately charmed by the place." He first came to the Southwest while a major in the military and decided to stay. "I knew I'd never go back to New York."

An avid gardener, with a two-story greenhouse, Murray continued to see patients every afternoon in his Canyon Road home. They called him a "miracle man."

"I decided I would find a method for treating pain beside morphine."

—*Murray Friedman*

Eve Gentry

THE EMBODIMENT OF CREATIVE VITALITY

I ALWAYS WANTED TO DANCE, but I was such a shy child that I never told anyone," said Eve Gentry. "I was also very skinny, and I wouldn't eat. My mother decided that maybe if I took dancing, I'd get an appetite. She didn't realize I was going to get an appetite to dance."

The youngest of five children, Henrietta Greenhood was born in Los Angeles in 1909. She took the professional name Eve Gentry in 1942, on marrying her childhood friend, Bruce Gentry, a printer and publisher. Eve's parents both left Europe as teenagers in the 1880s and met when her father came to the door selling Singer sewing machines. They married in Buffalo, New York and moved to Los Angeles and later San Bernardino, California, because Eve's mother suffered from asthma.

Eve was eight when she began studying ballet, folk, and ballroom dancing "from a peroxide-dyed blonde, young girl from Hollywood," who came to San Bernardino on Saturdays, she said. "I decided I would be a dancer, although I had no idea what it meant to be a dancer. I'd never seen a real dancer. I just focused all of my attention on dancing."

She was in high school when an established Russian ballet teacher from Hollywood came to San Bernardino to teach a class and offered Eve a scholarship to come to Hollywood to live and study. Her parents didn't want their youngest child to leave home, so she took classes in Hollywood on Saturdays— until she refused to come home.

Two siblings were living in San Francisco, and her parents consented to a move. Eve became quite taken with modern dance and was teaching in Palo Alto when Martha Graham came to perform. Eve auditioned for Graham, who offered her a scholarship.

In October 1936, Eve arrived in New York. Her brother took her to Hanya Holm's studio, and Holm invited Eve to audition. She "started the very next day" and was a principal performer with the Hanya Holm Dance Company from 1936 to 1942. Eve directed her own dance company from 1944 to 1968.

With rehearsals often "from 6:00 A.M. to midnight or after," dancing took its toll on her knees and back, "and nearly ruined me for life." Doctors recommended surgery; but then Eve met Joseph Pilates, who had created and designed resistance control equipment "to align and centralize the body, to learn to breathe correctly, and not put undue stress on the body." After a lesson with him, I was free of pain for the first time in three years." Impressed with his knowledge, Eve studied and taught with Pilates for twenty-two years, developing the Eve Gentry Technique, a blending of work that she learned from Pilates, Hanya Holm, and Rudolph Laban.

The Gentrys came to Santa Fe in 1968. Eve opened a dance studio on Camino de Monte Sol. She danced and choreographed for the Santa Fe Opera and trained opera apprentices for a number of years. And she brought the Pilates method to Santa Fe. In New York, her subtle exercises helped dancers acquire a competitive edge in speed or strength. In Santa Fe, they did wonders for plain folks with backaches. In the best dance world tradition, she trained the next generation of Pilates instructors, and founded the Physicalmind Institute, to insure the continuity of this healing work.

"I believe one
can dance
forever."
—*Eve Gentry*

Pauline Gomez

TEACHER WITH SPECIAL SIGHT

W HEN PAULINE GOMEZ RETURNED HOME to New Mexico after completing a graduate program at Harvard on scholarship, she couldn't find a job.

The year was 1946, and even though Pauline had distinguished herself as the first blind person to graduate from the University of New Mexico, "it was unusual for a blind person to get a job," she recalls.

Born in Moriarty in 1933 and raised in Santa Fe, Pauline had been blind since childhood. Hardly one to let discouragement stand in her way, the vital, articulate Pauline listened closely when she heard a friend complain about the lack of nursery schools in Santa Fe. "Open a kindergarten," her friend advised.

On October 1, 1946, in the back room of her home, Pauline did just that. Her Los Niños Kindergarten opened with just eight students. She operated the school and taught there thirty-five years.

"I'd always loved children," she recalls. "I used to work with neighborhood children when I was in high school." And children responded. "Miss Gomez can see with her ears," they said.

Her handicap didn't get in her way in the classroom. "If you establish respect with children, you're going to get along fine. You need to establish your rules." Creative dramatics, which stresses the use of the senses, and science were the subjects she enjoyed teaching. With a tape recorder, she took notes on students' progress, priding herself on the long letters and detailed reports she wrote parents, using a regular typewriter.

Six years after Los Niños opened, Pauline decided to build her own schoolhouse. "Then we ran it like a competitive business," she says, "because we had to pay the mortgage."

Pauline is thankful for her supportive family. "I had a very unusual mother. She has been a great help to me all my life. She was kind of pushy, really. There was nothing I couldn't do. She would always say, 'I know you can do it.' The only thing I really can't do is drive a car."

An active crusader in the blind movement both in-state and around the country, Pauline has worked long and hard to persuade legislators to eliminate discrimination against the blind. She became an active member of the National Federation of the Blind in 1956. She does volunteer work for the State Library.

"Blind people should be given every opportunity to prove themselves, just like those who are sighted," she affirms. "I preach this philosophy day and night."

"The purpose of teaching is to open your mind and stimulate curiosity." She certainly has opened the minds of generations of Santa Fe youngsters, who will never forget the enthusiastic spirit of their kindergarten teacher and who will always remember how well she could "see" in spite of her handicap.

"I am a crusader---a soldier in the front lines."   —*Pauline Gomez*

Telesfor Goodmorning

RAISING BLUE CORN AND WHITE CORN

IN THIS LAND OF SACRED MOUNTAINS, singing streams, count-less stars in the sky, where sunset is a nightly work of art, in the place of the Pueblo People, we have been privileged by the presence of elders among us.

"Elders who taught us how to pray, to sing songs to the plants, elders who laughed and cried, and who unselfishly shared their visions—those to whom a listening ear had no particular color, no race, no religion more important than any other, and whose thoughts were generational, not racial. Elders who knew and practiced the legacy of tradition being passed down the generations. Teles Goodmorning was such a gentle elder and great teacher,"* wrote Taos photographer Gail Russell about her good friend Telesfor Goodmorning.

Telesfor Reyna Goodmorning was born in 1900. "When I was a kid, we used to live up in the [Taos] Pueblo village. That's where I was born," said Telesfor. "I grew up with my brother, Manuel. My dad used to carry the plow on his shoulder. We had one horse, and we used to plow the south side of the pueblo. My father, Elkhorn, plowed blue corn, white corn, and yellow corn. I would go with him. Toward the middle of the day, my mother would go up there and fix some lunch, and we would eat."

As a young adult, Telesfor found himself doing a variety of jobs. "I worked on farms, down in the valley," he said. "In the 1920s, I worked cowboy jobs. I used to work where it is very popular now—at Angel Fire and Eagle's Nest. There's a lot of people in that valley they call Eagle's Nest today. There's an old trail that goes straight up from Eagle's Nest to the [Taos] Pueblo. I used to go over there on horseback in the summertime. It used to take me a little while to ride over." Telesfor also worked for fifteen years as a hunting guide in Texas.

A lieutenant war chief at the pueblo, Telesfor enjoyed traveling to powwows as a dancer, said former Taos Pueblo Governor Tony Reyna. He also traveled to Washington, D.C. to meet with President Roosevelt, campaigning to save the pueblo's sacred Blue Lake. "We went to the White House, Smithsonian Institution, and to the Congress," said Telesfor. In addition, he accepted an invitation to bless the chapel at the United Nations in New York City.

Telesfor and his wife, Pauline, raised three children, Jimmy, Esther, and Priscilla. In 1982, Jimmy was a participant in a Seed Banks Workshop in Tucson, Arizona. He took ears of his family's native blue corn, grown by his father, to the conference. "That's when blue corn got popular," said Telesfor.

At the time of his passing at the age of ninety-three, Gail Russell wrote the following poem to honor her dear friend Telesfor:

Bright Star of the Morning

When the sunflowers
and chamisa were
brilliantly golding the landscape
When the blue-purple star-faced
wild asters
were clear and true
On the morning when we awoke
and the first snow of winter
covered Mother Mountain with a
shining shawl
That day
he crossed over.
May he be in
Harmony, Beauty, and delight.
Wherever he is,
the Other Side has a Bright
Shining Star of the Morning.*

* From an article by Gail Russell in the Santa Fe *Sun*,
October 1993.

Shirley and Mary Greene

ECCLESIASTICAL "BUREAUCRAT" AND PIONEER WOMAN MINISTER

"Mary's history has been a history of taking small, struggling churches and then building them up," said Shirley Greene. Shirley's real strength is "as an organizer and program planner," said Mary Greene. "That was where we needed to have his energies."

Mary was ordained as a minister in the Congregational Church (now the United Church of Christ) over forty years ago, which makes her something of a pioneer. "I always knew if I'd been a boy, I'd be an ordained minister...I know what it is to be shut out. I was ordained back in the days before women were being ordained."

Born in Portland, Oregon in 1915, Mary lost her father early. Her mother was left with eight young children to raise. There was no money for college. Mary was thirty by the time she graduated from Pacific University.

She was the only woman preparing for the ministry at the Oberlin Graduate School of Theology in Ohio. Even before she'd taken her degree, she was called to serve a small congregation in tiny Craig, Colorado. It gave her a chance, she recalls, "to try out whether or not I could be a pastor. A woman minister was quite a novelty. People came to church out of curiosity."

Single until age forty-eight, she served the remote Colorado parishes, "where men with families couldn't afford to go." She lived in a trailer provided by the church. She married Shirley Greene in 1964 and the two ministers moved to St Louis. Shirley was born in 1911 in Hill, New Hampshire, to Arthur and Gertrude Greene. His parents wanted him to become minister of a fundamentalist congregation, but Shirley received his

doctor of divinity from the "liberal Chicago Theological Seminary," where he majored in social ethics. "Most of my career has been as what I have frequently referred to as an ecclesiastical bureaucrat," he said. Ordained in 1936, he served most of his career with the national and world ministries of the United Church of Christ. He also worked for the National Council of Churches for several years, as well as the United Methodist Board of Global Ministries' National Division, focusing on issues of rural economic development.

The Greenes moved to Santa Fe in 1981 and helped to establish the United Church of Santa Fe. Shirley got involved in legislative advocacy. "I was a lobbyist for the New Mexico Conference of Churches, organizing a series of issues and statements to advocate views and issues on human welfare," he said. He was instrumental in getting the Hunger Walk, an ecumenical, church-sponsored effort to raise funds to alleviate world hunger, started in Santa Fe. He also helped bring Habitat for Humanity to New Mexico and said, "Whereas Mary was the perennial pastor, I was the perennial bureaucrat/organizer."

When the couple moved to Santa Fe, Mary found that her volunteer work was "in people-related things." She initiated ecumenical services for nursing home residents, organized a Sunday evening ministry, and helped to establish the Visitor's Hospitality Center at the New Mexico State Prison.

"What I want to do is grow old gracefully," Mary says. "It's not easy. That's, I think, what most of us try to do and want to do. And when you do, you're witness to those around you."

"I chose what I wanted to do, and I did it— against a lot of odds."

—Mary Greene

Tino Griego

COACHING FROM A WHEELCHAIR

ONE OF SANTA FE'S UNIQUE BELOVED FIGURES, Augustine "Tino" Griego was born in 1927 and grew up along Palace Avenue. Playing football and baseball and building a swimming hole in the Santa Fe River in the summertime with all the other kids, Tino distinguished himself early as an athlete by winning a Golden Gloves championship.

"We had to make a hardball out of rags and tape," he recalled. "We were all poor, but it was a great neighborhood, and I had a lot of friends."

Tragically, by the time he was in his teens, Tino was crippled by arthritis and confined to a wheelchair for life. He could only watch the others play football and baseball. After the doctor told him, "You will never walk again," Tino "gave up." But through the persistence of his friends, who visited him every day, he began going out again, playing catch from his wheelchair.

In 1947, he was asked to supervise a city youth center in his neighborhood. Reluctantly, he took the job as director of the Palace Avenue Youth Center at 827 East Palace on a one-month trial basis. Generations of kids later, he was still at it—encouraging and coaching the thousands of young people who came to his center. One by one, he added activities—Ping-Pong, basketball, horseshoes, a punching bag. Decades later, he said, "I'm still working for peanuts, but I'm happy and I love what I do."

For many years, Tino kept to a rugged schedule of running the center for seventy-five kids all day, leaving at 4:00 P.M. to go coach the Little League teams, then returning to the center at 7:30 P.M. to keep it open until 10:00 P.M. "I'd rather see them here than out on the streets," he said. He learned how to coach from a wheelchair, and he provided the children of Santa Fe with a safe, comfortable place to shoot pool, compete at board games, play basketball, and watch videos.

Tino's work with the city's children is highly regarded and recognized. He is a recipient of the New Mexico Chapter of the National Council of Christians and Jews' Brotherhood Award, as well as many awards from the city of Santa Fe and the Santa Fe Police Department. In addition, the city honored him by naming one of its swimming pools after him.

When kids would say to him, "I wish I had a car, but my parents are too poor to afford one for me," he would tell them, "You're a rich kid. You have your health, and you can get around."

Tino once described the purpose of the center in this way: "The youth center gives the kids a place to go, keeping them out of trouble. The kids know me pretty well. They respect me and I respect them. I need to show the kids that life is worth living and that life is not always easy."*

---

* Dennis Rudner, "Tino Keeps the Faith Working for Kids," *Albuquerque Journal North*, n.d.

"I would never retire. I love the kids too much. I'll stay as long as I can push this wheelchair around."   —Tino Griego

Jim & Ruth Hall

TAKING THE REINS

⌖

J IM HALL JR. REMEMBERS HIS FATHER as a giant of a man. He had a"forty-six inch chest and a thirty inch waist," and "looked like a cowboy."Jim Hall Sr. was a Presbyterian minister, deeply involved in Christian education in the Southwest in the 1950s. He inherited his looks and and his calling from his father, Ralph Hall, a cowboy missionary who "rode the countryside on horseback and then in old cars, bringing the word of God to the ranches and outlying areas in the New Mexico territory."

With his father on the road all the time, Jim Hall Sr., the oldest of three children growing up in Albuquerque, "took on a lot of responsibility pretty early. When he was twelve," his son relates, "he took a schoolteacher out to the Navajo Reservation and drove back, a round trip of 250 miles." He studied for two years at McCormick Theological Seminary in Chicago. He married Ruth Hall, of Fort Davis Texas — who shared his birth date, May 3, 1918— and whisked her off to Ketchikan, Alaska, where he was pastor of a mission church for three years.

In Ketchikan he worked in the fishing industry. In San Francisco,in 1944, he worked in the shipyards while finishing seminary. His first churches were in Morenci, Arizona, Arlington, Texas and Hobbs, New Mexico, where he worked in the oil fields. All that hard outdoor work and varied pastoral experience prepared him for the assignment of his life: running Ghost Ranch.

In the 1950s it was just another ranch, at Abiquiu, in Georgia O'Keeffe country, when its owner, Arthur N. Pack,

deeded the property—complete with buildings, livestock, machinery, and mineral development rights—to the Presbyterian Board of Education. In 1961 Jim Hall took over the reins of the 23,000 acre spread. In twenty-five years as director of Ghost Ranch, he turned it into a popular conference center, while his wife, an ardent paleontologist, laid the groundwork for a small museum.

"My father could ride, "Jim Hall Jr. reminisces. " He could drive anything that had an engine in it, and he was the best shot I ever saw. He was just outstanding with his hands but he was also very much an intellectual. He could read Greek and Hebrew, and spoke passable French. He built Ghost Ranch into a nationally known camp and conference center. Ghost Ranch was and is a good neighbor to the surrounding ranches and farms, because it was important to him."

Ruth, the minister's wife, "came into her own at Ghost Ranch. She led paleontology seminars, and was a really gracious hostess, complementing my father," says her son. She hiked the surrounding mesas in search of fossils. Although she considered herself a mere amateur, she discovered the six-foot alligator-like skeleton of a phytosaur, which she reassambled "in an apparatus she set up in the garage." The phytosaur now resides at the Ruth Hall Paleontology Museum at Ghost Ranch, founded to house her fascinating finds from the Triassic period.

"Ghost Ranch is like my father in some ways—a mixture of the old and the new, the deeply intellectual and the practical. That's part of the magic of the place."   —*Jim Hall, Jr.*

Rosalie Heller

SETTING THE TONE FOR NORTHERN NEW MEXICO MUSIC

Her music professors at Brooklyn College were not happy when Rosalie Heller informed them that she wanted to head west. "They thought it was a musical wasteland—nobody to play music with and nobody to listen. My professors felt that I wouldn't be able to fulfill my potential," she said.

Born in Brooklyn, New York, in 1931, the daughter of Faye and Martin Liebschutz, Rosalie grew up with her brother, Arthur, five years her senior. "He was very important in my life. The first time I heard the Brahms's *First Symphony* he was playing it on his record player," said Rosalie. "I was just a little tiny girl. I thought it was the most wonderful sound I had ever heard in my life. My mother played the piano. She gave me my first music lessons. We had a big upright piano and a stool that turned."

Rosalie's big brother was also very interested in science. "The day the news was released that the atom bomb had been dropped, Arthur came running inside with a newspaper and said, 'They've split the atom. They dropped the bomb, and they built it in Los Alamos—the Secret City,'" said Rosalie. "My romantic self said, 'I want to go there. I want to live there,' and that began my love affair with Los Alamos."

During her youth in Brooklyn, Rosalie studied piano with a number of teachers. At the age of sixteen, she began to teach piano herself while attending James Madison High School.

Rosalie was pursuing a degree in music at Brooklyn College when she met Leon Heller, a physics major. After Rosalie graduated, she married Leon in 1952 and moved to Ithaca, New York, to do graduate work.

The Hellers moved to Los Alamos in 1956, and raised two sons and a daughter: Peter, Anthony, and Jean. "It was like a dream come true," Rosalie remembers. "I had read everything that I could get my hands on about Los Alamos—there wasn't too much at that time, but what I read fascinated me. I arrived in Los Alamos and loved it.

It took a while until the children were older before she could practice again at a serious level. Los Alamos piano students began studying with Rosalie in 1957. Although she started with "just a few students," she soon found that all of her teaching slots were full.

Rosalie cofounded the Los Alamos Arts Council in 1965. And she has chaired the artist selection committee for the Los Alamos Concert Association for many years. "Leon has always supported the hectic nature of my life," she said.

Of particular interest to Rosalie is the work of women composers. "Music by women really only became available in the early 1970s," she points out. "Until that point, it was very difficult to find music composed by women. If it had been published, it was out of print. We've done ourselves a disservice by not having performed it through the years."

In 1979, Rosalie cofounded and became manager of a popular chamber music series, The Coffeehouse, which presents New Mexico and out-of-state musicians performing in a coffeehouse setting. "I hope we've given people a wider appreciation of chamber music through the concerts," Rosalie said. "I am eternally grateful to Los Alamos."

"Through teach-
ing music, I hope
that I have given
my students . . .
a curiosity, a joy
[about] an art
form which has
shaped my life."
—Rosalie Heller

John Hightower

ELICITING TRUST AT THE HIGHEST LEVEL

JOHN HIGHTOWER CAME TO SANTA FE late in life, bringing his global reputation as a journalist. As a reporter for the Associated Press wire service, he covered all the major events of the post World War II era: the founding of the United Nations, the Marshall Plan, the Japanese Peace conference, the North Atlantic Treaty negotiations, the Kennedy-Khruschev summit of 1961. Not bad for a coal miner's son from Tennessee. But no one who knew him was surprised at his trajectory.

Born in 1909 in Coal Creek, Tennessee, John attended Knoxville public schools and the University of Tennesee. He left after two years to work as a reporter for the Knoxville News Sentinel. At the Associated Press in Nashville, from 1933, he was quickly promoted to Tennessee state editor. In 1936 his coverage of Democratic and Republican national conventions caught the attention of the Washington AP Bureau Chief, who brought the young newsman to Washington. John became known for in depth,explanatory-interpretive reporting.

At the height of the Korean War in 1952, John won the Pulitzer Prize (and two other major awards) for "the sustained quality of his coverage of news of international affairs." The Pulitzer committee praised in particular John's prescient coverage of events that led President Truman to remove General Douglas MacArthur, from command in Korea. MacArthur was ready to expand the war into Communist China. Truman was not. Hightower's reporting reassured readers the country was not on the brink of World War III.

In 1938 John married Martha Nadine Joiner, of New York City. They were married forty one years and had three children.

The journalist's first Santa Fe connection was anthropologist Edward Hall, who got to know the Hightowers while working for the State Department in Washington in the 1950s. They became close friends. "John knew and was consulted by all the Secretaries of State and was trusted clear up to the president," Hall recalls. "He was unusually intelligent, perceptive and modest. He was conscientious and consistent. He had a tremendous reputation among news people for being completely trustworthy....He was highly dedicated to his work—there wasn't anything else in his life, really."

On his retirement from the AP in 1971, John and his wife joined the Halls in Santa Fe. He taught journalism at UNM and contributed a weekly Sunday op-ed page column to the Santa Fe New Mexican. To New Mexican columnist, David Roybal, Hightower was a mentor, a close friend and a great history teacher. "I went to public school in this state, and the university. But I learned more about Averell Harriman, Harry Truman, Dwight Eisenhower, from editing his column." The older journalist's work habits made a deep impression on Roybal. "After his column appeared in the paper, he would read it all over again, to make sure it was edited correctly and because, experienced as he was, he was always searching for a better way to say something."

"My aim is to strive for under-standing."

—*John Hightower*

Allan Houser

FATHER OF CONTEMPORARY INDIAN SCULPTURE

Since 1984, WHEN THE AWARD WAS CREATED, the National Medal of Arts has gone to a dozen luminaries each year, Georgia O'Keefe, Marian Anderson, Ella Fitzgerald and Aaron Copeland among them. In 1992 it went to Allan Houser, the sculptor whose works—monumental, intimate and steepedin history —are at home everywhere from the Smithsonian in Washington to the Pompidou Museum in Paris. He was the first Native American to win the award. Some might say it was long overdue.

A Chiricahua Apache, Allan was born on his parents' government-grant farm in Apache, Oklahoma in 1914, as the tribe was emerging from twenty-seven years as US prisoners of war,in forced exile from their native mountains in the Southwest. Allan's father, Sam Haozous, was captured with Geronimo in 1886, and later served as the great chief's interpreter. Allan grew up listening to his father play the drum, sing medicine songs and tell the stories of Geronimo.

In 1934, Allan came to Santa Fe to study art at the Santa Fe Indian School, changing his name from Haozous (which means "the sound of pulling roots") to Houser. "Dorothy Dunn was the first teacher I had." Allan studied painting, but he "wanted more," and said, "I had something else in mind when I came here. I didn't want to do Indian-style paintings. I didn't care for it at all, but that was the only way that I could get into the arts." Dunn objected to some of the things Allan wanted to do, and told her student, "We don't do that here." In 1962, when Allan became a teacher at the Institute of American Indian Arts, his students heard a different message. "We do everything." Allan met his wife of more than fifty years, the former Anna Marie Gallegos of Abiquiu, in Santa Fe. Allan and Anna Marie raised five sons.

Allan received his first commission for a sculpture in 1949 from the Haskell Institute in Lawrence, Kansas—a memorial in stone of Indian servicemen killed in World War II. He later received a Guggenheim grant in sculpture and painting. "When I won my Guggenheim fellowship, I said I wanted to become one of the best—whether painter or sculptor—in the world. That's what my efforts are going to be, whether I get there or not," he said.

"Allan taught a whole generation of new Indian artists," said Robert Breunig, former chief curator of the Heard Museum in Phoenix. "I think we can safely say he is the father of contemporary Indian sculpture."

Many artists have copied his work. "I think it's a shame because I taught them not to be that way. I taught them to be individuals," Allan lamented. "Be yourself. Be respectful of yourself. Don't look around too much and see what other guys are doing. There are too many looking around and seeing people that are selling things. They want to jump on the bandwagon and copy that particular style."

His style fused European modernist influences—Arp, Brancusi, Moore—with Oklahoma childhood memories of Indians from many tribes, dressed proudly in traditional style. He liked to work in stone, he told the makers of a 1992 TV tribute, because stone is part of the earth, and he came from people who think they are part of the earth. And because stone lasts forever.

Anna Marie, Roy, Stephen & Lon Houser, Phillip & Bob Haozous

"You look inside.
You experiment.
You explore.
You do things
that are differ-
ent."

—*Allan Houser*

Harmon & Cornelia Hull

BUILDING COMMUNITY

CORNELIA HULL IS COMPILING A BOOK of her husband's wartime letters home. "Harmon tried to write four or five times a week, so it's a historical document," she told us. During the Second World War, her husband, a physician, served in the China, Burma, India theater. He headed a hospital at Kwei-Lin that was destroyed by the Japanese.

Harmon and Cornelia Hull met in Galveston, Texas, where both were studying medicine. Harmon was born in 1903 in Fairwater, Wisconsin; Cornelia in 1904 in Chautauqua County, New York. They married in 1930. Harmon completed his residency in Richmond, Virginia. They settled in Wisconsin and raised four sons: Pieter, Bruce, Stephen, and Douglas.

Harmon was a general practitioner, a charter member of the Academy of Family Practice. Cornelia, her medical studies sidetracked by the Depression and the war, threw her energies into community work — school board, League of Women Voters, and the Waupan Council on Human Relations. Organized by League members, the Council was a community (as opposed to church) effort on behalf of migrant workers. "We understood," Cornelia says, "that it was the first community project of its kind... in the country."

Mexican-Americans from the Texas border arrived in the Waupan area each spring to work in the sugar beet fields and stayed right through the fall before moving on to the orchards of the Northwest. Their children never saw the inside of a school, until Cornelia and colleagues got going. They opened a pioneer bilingual school, staffed by Spanish speaking students from University of Wisconsin; they started health and housing programs and opened the local swimming pool to migrant families. Cornelia also served on the Governor's Commission on Human Rights, under four Wisconsin governors.

The Hulls moved to Santa Fe in 1968. Disturbed by the lack of affordable housing in his new community, Harmon bought a few old condemned houses on the west side. "He thought we should renovate them, make them attractive, and then have the people who had been living in them before be able to move back in without having to pay more rent. It was his little personal Habitat for Humanity."

Cornelia also continued her community service in Santa Fe. She proposed to the Santa Fe League of Women Voters that a farmers market be started. "We realized that one of the problems with housing for low income people in town was that many of them couldn't make a living on their farms." As families moved into town to live with relatives, "houses were getting overcrowded. . . . We thought that if they had a market for the produce, they might be able to make ends meet a little better. I did much of the groundwork," and today the farmers market continues "to be a thriving institution."

When the Hulls learned that there was interest in starting a new church, they joined with others to found the United Church of Santa Fe.

The Hulls also helped found a neighborhood association, Los Vecinos, to prevent development in their historic district. "It was the very first one that was formed in the city," Cornelia recalled.

"It's a wonderful life—full of opportunities. Don't be afraid to try out new things and have new experiences."

—*Cornelia Hull*

Bill Isaacs

ADVOCATE FOR MOTHER NATURE

IF YOU HAVE ANY INTEREST IN THE PLANT LIFE and biodiversity of northern New Mexico, you will inevitably come in contact with the Native Plant Society of New Mexico, the Nature Conservancy, the Audubon Society, the horticulture program at Santa Fe Community College, and the Santa Fe Botanical Garden. All these organizations have benefited from the energy and guidance of Santa Fe botanist and teacher Bill Isaacs.

Inheriting two green thumbs, Bill was born in 1938 in Medford, Oregon, with a gardener grandmother on one side of the family and a Rogue River farmer grandfather on the other. By the time he was fifteen, he had discovered his passion for mycology and decided "this was something he really wanted to do." By 1963 he was hunting for mushrooms in the mountains outside Santa Fe, "getting close to the land and spending time hiking and looking."

Weaving his way between academia and the "real" world, Bill taught first at the College of Santa Fe, then Santa Fe Community College. Later he worked in state government with the Natural Resources Department and as a nursery botanist. Since 1971 Bill has been developing courses that provide an understanding of environmental issues as well as knowledge of the natural world. He has pioneered courses such as Mushroom Identification, Bird Identification, Bioremediation, Plant Identification, the Natural History of New Mexico, and Xeriscape Gardening, courses he has taught at Santa Fe Community College..

Bill received his bachelor of science and master's degrees from the University of Washington. He also did advanced graduate studies in botany at the University of Michigan.

Known for his "wild field trips," Bill has trained dozens of area landscapers and gardeners. "It's said that the requirements for my field trips are a pair of binoculars and a fast car," he remarks.

"The thing that motivates it all," he says, "is a consuming interest in how it works. The natural world fascinates me. Even though you don't understand all of it, you get wonderful insights that are like new universes. As you get older, your reach is greater. Suddenly, you're not doing disciplines—you're seeing how things work!"

Over the years, Bill has had the experience of witnessing the effects of his work. While he believes the climate is changing "dramatically fast" and becoming drier, he is demonstrating alternative ways of caretaking plants. Since he began teaching in 1971 he has seen "an enormous sea change" in the public's interest and degree of sophistication. Meanwhile, he continues to invent ways "we can mitigate bad tendencies and bring forth ideas to restore natural systems and identify problems."

Bill's love of plant life has led him to advocate on behalf of growing things, in such groups as Citizens for Clean Air and Water, the National Wildlife Federation, and the Santa Fe Land Use Advisory Committee. Botanist, activist, naturalist, and environmentalist—these roles only begin to explain Bill's enormous influence on the way people in Santa Fe think about their environment.

"I am completely dedicated to life."   —*Bill Isaacs*

John B. Jackson

GEOGRAPHER OF THE WEST

VERY QUIETLY, FROM 1951 TO 1970 John Brickerhoff (J. B.) Jackson published a magazine in Santa Fe that had worldwide impact. Called *Landscape,* this magazine circulated around the world, transmitting the ideas and vision of its creator and publisher, a keen observer of both man-made and natural environments. As one who paid close attention to the roads, the irrigation ditches, the designs of towns and living environments, John began the publication with the notion of "arousing a kind of speculative interest in the human geography of the Southwest."

Born in Paris in 1910, John was educated at boarding schools in Europe and lived on the East Coast. He first visited New Mexico in 1926, when, as a young man, he spent time on his uncle's sheep ranch in Wagon Mound. "I wanted to be a rancher," he said, but instead he became a teacher of the history of the American landscape, at Harvard, the University of California at Berkeley, the University of Minnesota, and the University of New Mexico. His ideas and publications formed the core of a new curriculum of "landscape studies," which developed as the students he influenced went on to teach their students. John has made his home in New Mexico since 1945, living in Pojoaque and at Las Golondrinas before moving into his home in La Cienega.

Not that John didn't try his hand at ranching—he did, at Cimarron before World War II and at Clines Corners afterward. During the war, as a combat intelligence officer in France, he discovered his future profession. "I had to find the character of the countryside," he said, "and I became interested in geography. That led to reading, which led to writing." While in France, he had the opportunity to study books in the fine old libraries, where, he said, he "learned a way of seeing the land."

John's books, *Landscapes, The Necessity for Ruins,* and *Discovering the Vernacular Landscape,* became classics in the field. Then, in 1995, the writers' organization PEN honored him for his essay collection, *A Sense of Place, A Sense of Time,* with its Spielvogel-Diamondstein Award for the Art of the Essay.

His keen eye catches what the rest of us take for granted:roads, irrigation ditches, field patterns, and imprints on the land. He sees political significance in the straightline grid of city streets, suburban lawns, and barbed wire fences. "Each space," he wrote, " is unique and can in fact affect the activity taking place within it."

John was also known for his recognition of "vernacular" space; mobile homes, for example, which he writes about in his essay "Wheel Estate: Mobile Homes on the Range." In order to see what is really around us, he suggests, we must learn to look without judgment.

"The contemporary American landscape . . . the streets and houses and fields and places of work, teach us a great deal not only about American society but also about ourselves and how we relate to the world."

—*John B. Jackson*

Bill & Julie James

BRINGING PEOPLE TOGETHER

⚭

THE WALLS OF JULIE JAMES'S EL CASTILLO APARTMENT provide a glimpse of two artists, who, for half a century, shared their lives and their love of painting. "Bill painted these portraits and abstracts," Julie said. "This is the portrait he painted of our daughter, Sara. Bill's work was exhibited in a small gallery in Woodstock, Vermont."

Bill and Julie met as neighbors in Vermont and married in 1945. Julie's two sons, from a previous marriage, David and John Borden and three children of their own, Nathaniel (known as Spook), Sara and Jemima made for a large and lively household, passionate about painting, music, storytelling and entertaining. It was a rich and fulfilling life.

The family shared another interest —dowsing, the search for hidden objects by means of a forked divining rod or a pendulum, that swings significantly in reply to well phrased questions. Bill learned this ancient skill from "an old country man back in New Hampshire, and used it to find objects friends had lost. "More often than not it worked," according to Julie.

The grandson of philosopher William James and great-nephew of author Henry James, William ("Bill") James was born in Boston, Massachusetts, in 1913. "I lived in New England—Massachusetts and New Hampshire—for the first years of my life," he said. "I went to a lot of different schools, which maybe was a mistake because you never got continuity." He attended Le Rosey School in Switzerland, the Lenox School in Massachusetts, Exeter in New Hampshire, and graduated from the Fountain Valley School in Colorado Springs. "I never was anywhere where I felt so at home and comfortable as in the Rocky Mountains. I loved it. I came down to Santa Fe twice

to visit—in 1931 and 1932—to see what it was like." Bill also studied art at the Boston Museum School of Fine Art and at the American Academy in Rome.

Julie was born Juliana Holden in 1913 in Old Bennington, Vermont. "My mother, Florence, was a housewife and mother," she said. Her father, Clarence Holden, founded the Bennington Scale Company, but the business folded. "Despite the business setback, we had a wonderfully secure childhood. The world was a different place in those days."

Julie's interest in art was kindled early, by her grandmother, a plein air painter, who took her eight year old granddaughter along on excursions in search of a motif. Julie was allowed to carry the paintbox and given small canvasses to daub. After boarding school in Providence,R.I., she studied at Bennington College, in their first ever art classes.

Bill and Julie moved to Santa Fe from Aspen, Colorado, in 1968 and soon developed a reputation as gracious hosts. "I enjoyed cooking and bringing people together," Julie said. "Bill enjoyed telling stories and singing songs. He could remember all the songs, poetry, and stories that he knew when he was young. In later years, nobody could bring up a subject but what he had a song to match it."

When he lost a couple of fingers in a compost grinder accident, and had to give up his beloved banjo, his children bought him a violin at a hock shop. "Bill became fascinated with the shape of the violin and the construction, and began making violins with no more than books to give him ideas," Julie recalled. He built twenty-two violins, five violas and a cello.

"One of the things we enjoyed most was being with our friends. . . . It would bring out sides of us that we didn't see every day."

—*Julie James*

Myra Ellen Jenkins

NEW MEXICO'S INDOMITABLE HISTORIAN

As STATE HISTORIAN, TEACHER, SCHOLAR, AND FRIEND, Myra Ellen Jenkins was an independent-thinking individual whose forthright opinions and feisty wit made an unforgettable impact on all those she met. From 1960 until her retirement in 1980, she served as state archivist and as New Mexico's first state historian, making her reputation as the final authority on New Mexico history. Governor Bruce King called her "the most knowledgeable person in New Mexico about the state's history."

No ivory tower historian, "Dr. J." frequently served as expert historical witness who brought her knowledge of land grants into disputes on complex land and water rights issues entangled in three centuries of Spanish, Mexican, and American documents. Her 1974 book, *A Brief History of New Mexico*, co-authored with Al Schroeder, is still considered the most complete introduction to the state's history. A great defender and protector of New Mexico's heritage, she was responsible for keeping many documents within the state.

Born in 1916 and reared on a ranch in the Black Forest area near Colorado Springs, she earned two degrees in European history at the University of Colorado, then taught history in the public schools of Pueblo for ten years.

"I can't remember when I wasn't interested in history of some sort," she said. "My grandfather had brought across from England a set of English history books. I used to sit upstairs at the farm and pore through them by the hour."

After earning her Ph.D. at the University of New Mexico's Latin American Institute, she worked for the Museum of New Mexico. In 1960 it fell to her to order the chaos of state historical documents. She rescued such priceless papers as the 1695 journals of Don Diego de Vargas, which had suffered water damage under a leaky roof in the Palace of the Governors.

"The first job was to clear out every cubbyhole, nook, and cranny of the old Roundhouse," she said. "Many documents had been put out for wastepaper."

Notoriously contemptuous of New Mexico's most famous historical character, Billy the Kid, Myra Ellen claimed he was a "two-bit punk who didn't deserve all the attention." Colleagues loved to one-up each other with kitsch presents for the "Kid Junque" display in her office.

Her early love of animals on the ranch carried over to the beloved cats who shared her Don Cubero Street home, particularly her cat and "research assistant" Amos.

She remained as active as ever in retirement, teaching at the University of New Mexico and New Mexico State University, mentoring students, pursuing publication of her scholarly work, and serving on numerous boards, including those of the Historic Santa Fe Foundation, El Rancho de las Golondrinas, and the State Records Commission. In later years this frail, white-haired lady was responsible for saving a historic site in La Cienega and helping Taos Pueblo reclaim its sacred Blue Lake from the federal government.

"I might wear out, but damned if I'm going to rust out!" she exclaimed.

"Most people can't tell you the difference between an archive and an endive."   —*Myra Ellen Jenkins*

Bergere Kenney

BELOVED PHYSICIAN

SANTA FE NATIVE Bergere Kenney, whose family traces its roots in New Mexico to the time of the Spanish land grants, lived all his life in the town where he was born and raised. His contributions, both professional and cultural, changed the city forever, and helped to make it the mecca it is today.

Born in a little house on Don Gaspar Street in 1921—"not a log cabin though, nothing so quaint as that"—Bergere graduated from Santa Fe High School, received his bachelor's degree from Harvard, and went on to get a medical degree from Northwestern University. After a stint in the army, he returned to Santa Fe in 1948, to practice internal medicine and cardiology.*

The cardiac care unit Bergere set up in 1967 at St. Vincent Hospital is named in his honor. During the difficult time of transition for the hospital, when its supervision was transferred from the Catholic Sisters of Charity to the present nonsectarian administration, Bergere served as the hospital's chief of staff.* "If I were to look back with nostalgia on anything in my career, it would be that time," he said.

When the hospital outgrew its quarters on Palace Avenue, Bergere, along with hospital director Sister Mary Joaquin and Dr. Will Friedman, envisioned and brought into being the new hospital on St. Michael's Drive.

Bergere and his wife Dolores, a bacteriologist, raised five remarkable children. Science, medicine, music and community activism run in the family. Son David is a chemical engineer. Daughter Ellen is a nurse who worked closely with her father at St Vincent Hospital. Daughter Nancy is a musician, daughter Katie a Board member at the College of Santa Fe. Son Chris holds a Phd in anatomy and practises ophthalmology in California. At last count, there were ten Kenney grandchildren.

Bergere sang in the Harvard Glee Club under the direction of Igor Stravinsky and played the guitar. He always loved chamber music; he became the first local president of the Santa Fe Chamber Music Festival. The Kenneys often hosted visiting Festival musicians at their home, providing rehearsal and performance space as well. He remained a strong supporter, actively involved over the years.

His wife, Dolores, played piano. "Music was a bond between them," daughter Katie says.

Greatly beloved by patients and the entire community, Bergere and Dolores are also remembered for their participation in Fiesta de Santa Fe, the floats they built and the legendary Fiesta parties they held at their home. "Dad always chose home sites [on the basis] of whether he could see Zozobra," Katie remembers.

He was "a loving father, a very gentle, even-handed man who taught by example," says Katie. She has fond memories of him riding to his office on his bicycle, his doctor bag looped on the handlebar.

---

* K.C. Compton, "Doctor Who Did Much for City Receives His Due," *New Mexican*, February 20, 1988.

"Be quiet and listen. You can learn a lot more when you're listening than when you're talking."

—*Bergere Kenney*

John Kenney

LOVER OF THE LAND

A NATIVE SANTA FEAN DEDICATED TO SERVICE, after his retirement from a thirty-year distinguished military career, John Kenney returned to his hometown to become one of its leading conservationists.

Born in 1918, a descendant of New Mexico's venerable Luna and Otero families, John attended New Mexico Military Institute and Regis College before going on to West Point. He also earned his master's degree at UCLA, and completed studies at Harvard Graduate School of Business. He served in Europe during World War II and in the Korean War. During his career, he worked at the Pentagon, was assistant commandant at Fort Sill, Oklahoma, where he remained for thirteen years, and in 1966 attained the rank of brigadier general. One of his assignments was as hemisphere planner for the joint chiefs of staff.

During his military career, John was decorated many times, receiving four United States military decorations, two foreign decorations, and eight service medals. Immediately following his retirement in 1970 he became director of the first United States Postal Administration School at Norman, Oklahoma, where thousands of postal employees from around the nation received training. He headed Norman's United Way Fund Drive.

In 1980, John and his wife Josephine returned to the town where he was born and raised—Santa Fe. As an active hiker, camper, and fisherman, he joined the Sierra Club. He led the Rio Grande Chapter, and served as head of the Political Action Committee of the New Mexico Sierra Club. He was a highly effective spokesman on environmental issues. Clear-cutting of forests was a particular concern of his. He was active in the defense of the Carson and Santa Fe national forests. As Josephine says, "He was good at keeping the peace" and was gifted at facilitating discussion.

He served as a trustee of the Santa Fe Community Foundation and joined the Wilderness Society.

John's very active life after retirement was enhanced by the reunion with his brother, Santa Fe physician Bergere Kenney, and by frequent family gatherings of his five children and many grandchildren. Described by his wife as an "extremely religious" person, John regularly attended St. Francis Cathedral, a family tradition.

"He was an optimistic person," says Josephine, firm in the belief that problems have solutions.

In 1987, the Sierra Club honored him with its Susan E. Miller Award for "eighteen years of dedicated, dynamic leadership at every level of activity."

"To rest is to rust."   —*John Kenney*

Eleanor King

GRAND LADY OF DANCE

∽

"I HAVE BEEN ASKED WHAT WERE THE OBSTACLES I had to overcome in my dancing life. I had a lot of resistance to overcome with my family," Eleanor King recalled. "My parents were not at all impressed that I wanted to be a dancer; this was unheard of in my family. I had five brothers and sisters who all thought I was mad, and that in a way was a good . . . springboard, I guess. The more they objected, the more I was determined to do it."

A pioneer modern dancer and soloist with the Humphrey-Weidman Company during the early years of modern dance, Eleanor's career as a dancer and choreographer spanned six decades. Her repertory of more than one hundred dances was inspired by her lifelong study of the dances of other cultures.

Born in 1906 to Emma and George King, an engineer, in Middletown, Pennsylvania, Eleanor was ambitious in her youth. "I wanted to do everything. I wanted to paint and draw and dance and act, and in my own crude ways, I did all of those things."

The King family moved to Brooklyn in 1922. Eleanor went to see Anna Pavlova's farewell tour at the Metropolitan Opera House in 1923 and "went home and wrote a poem about the swan dying so silently." She graduated from Erasmus Hall High School in 1924 and began studying theater with Priscilla Robineau, who told Eleanor that to become a professional dancer she must study at the Denishawn School. In the fall of 1927 she enrolled, only to learn that "Ruth St. Denis and

Mr. Shawn and company were on tour." Doris Humphrey and Charles Weidman were in charge, but this turned out to work in her favor. "I didn't know how lucky I was . . . after three lessons with Doris, she invited me to be one of the purples in her new ballet called *Color Harmony*," Eleanor recalled.

Eleanor founded the Theatre Dance Company in 1935. *Icaro,* a large group work she choreographed, premiered at the Brooklyn Museum of Art in 1937, and won a Bennington Fellowship. *Ode to Freedom* was another major work.

While teaching at Perry-Mansfield, a summer dance camp in Steamboat Springs, Colorado, Eleanor was introduced to the folk dancing of mountain people. After returning to New York, she choreographed *The Hornpipe* to national acclaim.

In 1958, she traveled to Japan to study *Noh*. "The *Noh* play, to me, was the ideal form of theater." Eleanor returned to Japan in 1967 on a Fulbright grant. She was awarded a second Fulbright grant in 1976 to study Korean Shamana and Buddhist dance and drama.

She first saw Santa Fe in 1936, when the streets were unpaved and she "wanted to pat every adobe wall." She retired to Santa Fe in 1971. She may be the only modern dancer to have performed at the New Mexico State House. At the 1987 Governor's Awards ceremony, she danced her acceptance speech. Knees bent, back arched, arms flung wide, she declaimed to a delighted audience, "When I first saw New Mexico, I was sky-struck!"

"The young dancers are now wanting to get to know more about the roots of modern dance. Today, I can look back and see . . . people doing my early pieces, and doing them . . . much better technically than I ever could. . . . It's just a joy."
—*Eleanor King*

Norbert Kreidl

GLASS TECHNOLOGY EXPERT

"My main interest in all my life from my ninth year on was teaching—in the widest sense, working with smart young people," said glass scientist, lecturer/consultant, and teacher Norbert Kreidl. As a nine year old he "procured a syllabus on how to teach first grade."

Born in Vienna in 1904, Norbert completed his Ph.D. in physics in the late 1920s. Trained in Germany in the science and technology of glass, he worked in the glass industry in Czechoslovakia for ten years. He came to the United States in 1938 with his young wife, Melanie, to escape Hitler's reign of terror. They arrived "with thirteen dollars and a baby." Norbert got a job teaching at Pennsylvania State University.

In 1943, Norbert began working for Bausch and Lomb, becoming director of materials research and development. At age sixty-four, Norbert found himself "retired by force by the rules of industry that you are too senile to do research." So he taught college graduate students from his sixty-fifth to his seventy-second year. "In a way, I returned to teaching, except my students were graduate students instead of first graders."

The Kreidls moved to Santa Fe in 1974. Norbert considered the City Different "my city, my country, my home." Home, that is, when he wasn't traveling as a lecturer/consultant. In 1984, he "made about 150,000 miles," he said. Between 1986 and 1988 he was on assignment in Europe six times.

When an Egyptian graduate student studying at the University of Missouri couldn't find employment in the United States, Norbert obtained a fellowship so that he could study glass physics in his native country. While in Egypt to supervise his student, Norbert made the acquaintance of Salah Arafa, a professor at the American University in Cairo.

The two professors found themselves asking "What good do these Ph.D.s do for Egypt?" Norbert recalled. "Do they need glass physicists? Do they need Ph.D.s? . . . So we decided to approach Salah's ancestral village, Basaisa, and ask the people 'What do you want—not what do we bring—what do you want?'"

The two professors met with the adults and children of the village, and began "an intimate relationship of appropriate approach to appropriate technology in a village of three hundred Egyptians." The children voted for four priorities: writing and reading, English, furniture making, and football. Fifteen years later, "the village had ten cooperatives doing things like knitting and furniture making."

Thousands of visitors have come to Basaisa to learn how to imitate the network in other countries. People throughout the world became interested in the village project, and money was donated "to build a small building as a center for these activities." A library was added, with "primarily books for do-it-yourself projects and children's books."

Basaisa villagers named their library Kreidl-El Basousi Library, and Norbert traveled to Egypt for his namesake's dedication. He entered the village riding a black horse. It was the first horseback ride of his life—at age eighty-four.

"El Basousi means 'one from the village of Basaisa.'" —*Norbert Kreidl*

Jack & Marge Lambert

EXPLORERS OF TRAILS AND CULTURES

JACK AND MARGE LAMBERT—THE COWBOY and the anthropologist—stand out as the kind of memorable people who gave Santa Fe its special character.

Born in 1898 on a ranch near Ocarche, Oklahoma, Everett Vey Lambert, always known as "Jack," left home at fourteen to go cowboying in Wyoming, Utah, and on the 101 Ranch in Oklahoma. But when he found New Mexico, he found home. He and his brother bought the Bishop's Lodge in Santa Fe, where they ran a dude ranch. Later they ran pack trips out of Hacienda San Gabriel near Alcalde. Many easterners who fell in love with New Mexico and moved to Santa Fe, got their first look at the country with Jack as their guide, Mary Cabot Wheelwright and the White sisters included.

Remembering that time, Jack said, "There was no pavement and not one fence between here and Gallup or the Grand Canyon."

When Amelia and Martha White's DeVargas Development Company sold lots on 385 acres in the Garcia Street area, Jack supervised the road building. He became manager of the Whites' estate, now the School of American Research.

The first woman curator of archaeology in the United States, Marge Lambert, born in 1911, came from a family of Scottish Colorado pioneers. She first met Jack at a dance in a boxcar at Seton Village while she was a graduate student at the University of New Mexico. "I thought I was pretty sophisticated, but then, I'd never been to a Santa Fe party!

"When Jack was courting me, I lived in one of Mrs. McComb's historic chicken houses. He had a cream-colored roadster, and he'd drive me to picnic on the Pajarito Plateau where he took his dudes. He always looked so wonderful in his crisp, spotless khaki clothes, his big Stetson, and his polished boots! He'd cook roasting ears, steak and coffee for us, and through all the years he's taken me all over the Southwest, even to the Cody water tower where he woke up after his clash with apricot brandy."* The two were married in 1950.

"We went with everyone else in town to the Morangs' Saturday Nights for years, and I always think of their house as the 'West Bank of the Acequia Madre.' Alfred played his violin and Dorothy or John Sloan played the piano. I was a regular guest on Alfred's radio program and discussed Southwestern archaeology and history."*

Marge had planned to become a social worker, but "Once I got my hands in the dirt, I was sunk." A student of Edgar Lee Hewett, the first director of the Museum of New Mexico, Marge worked at the museum for forty years—as curator of archaeology, anthropology, exhibits, and research. During this time, she assembled and recorded the museum's considerable anthropology collection. As a young woman, she did early fieldwork at important sites such as Quarai, Gran Quivira, and Abó; Jemez; Chaco Canyon; and Paa'ko, the "first big excavation of which [she] was totally in charge," overseeing forty workmen and University of New Mexico students.

She published over one hundred papers and several books, while managing all the lectures for the museum.

"I don't know how I did it," she told us. "I just did."

---

* Marian F. Love, "An Anthropologist Meets a Cowboy," *The Santa Fean* (December 1981): 39.

"As a woman, you're expected to carry your own pack of rocks."

—*Marge Lambert*

"Even when there's no one around, you're never lonely if you have a fire to look into."

—*Jack Lambert*

Delfinio Lujan

MASTER OF REMEDIOS

THE CLOSING OF LUJAN'S PLACE IN 1991, the last locally-run general store downtown, marked the end of an era for many who know and love Santa Fe. Since 1968, Delfinio Lujan had served all those who walked through the door of his Galisteo Street store, supplying them with basic household needs—cast-iron skillets, kerosene lanterns, bridles, and ice cream bars. The shelves were crammed with the useful, everyday articles of living.

And although Delfinio refused the title of "Dr. Lujan," which so many wanted to call him, he was the town's expert on *remedios*, traditional herbal cures. He preferred to think of himself, and have others think of him, as a merchant rather than as healer. But in wooden bins along the wall of his store he stocked the healing herbs that so many of the older generation relied on, and which the younger generation was discovering. "The hippie girls were the best customers," he recalled.

Delfinio learned about the curative powers of herbs from the old people who came in. He would ask them about the herbs they bought, then write down their advice. "I know what these herbs are good for," he would say, and he didn't charge anything for his consultations. He remembered how, in the old days when his brother-in-law ran the general store, people would be waiting by the door on Monday mornings to sell the native herbs they had gathered over the weekend.

Delfinio's wealth of knowledge, his willingness to share it freely, his simplicity, sense of humor, and balance all made him one of the most beloved of Santa Fe's unique characters. He knew which herbs were good for arthritis, which improved vitality, and which could help you sleep at night.

Born near the pueblo of Santa Clara in the tiny village of Guachupangue in 1907, Delfinio worked in the mines in Telluride, Colorado, in his younger days. In 1930, he came to Santa Fe with his wife Frances and went to work for her brother, Mr. Roybal, in the Galisteo Street store. Every day, well into his eighties, he walked to work downtown from his home near the Masonic Temple above Washington Street. His personal prescription for health and longevity: "Having good work and a brisk walk to it."*

---

*From *Santa Fe Lifestyle* (Summer 1987).

"I'm a merchant.
Not a healer. It's
the herbs that do
that."*
–Delfinio Lujan

Detail from photograph on pages ii–iii.

William Lumpkins

ARTIST, ARCHITECT, ACTIVIST

THE TERM "RENAISSANCE MAN" is much overused. William Lumpkins truly earns the name. Architect, artist, solar energy pioneer, author, student of Zen Buddhism, community and political activist—William Lumpkins has been an important influence in Santa Fe for seventy years. Who else has a grand ballroom at the La Fonda Hotel named for him?

Born in 1909 on the Rabbit Ears Ranch near Clayton, New Mexico, to a pioneering family, he realized early in life that ranching was not for him. As a young man, he had for friends and mentors artist Peter Hurd and writer Paul Horgan, whom he met when his family relocated to Lincoln County and he was attending Roswell High School. At Capitan in 1935, he built his first passive solar house.

Young William made his first trip to Santa Fe in 1927 with friend Peter Hurd; later, as a graduate of the University of New Mexico School of Architecture, he designed over two thousand buildings in Santa Fe, including DeVargas Center and Rancho Encantado. Merging modern technology with ancient adobe building techniques, William was responsible for many historic preservation projects in town. Notably the restoration of the Santuario de Guadalupe.

With other solar activists, in 1972 William founded Sun Mountain Design, an influential group responsible for the solar demonstration center at Ghost Ranch, north of Santa Fe. He was an innovator with the photo voltaic cell, which converts solar energy to electricity, and an advocate of other renewable energy sources, such as the hot dry rock application

A noted watercolorist, William has been associated with the major art movements of New Mexico in this century. As one of the Transcendentalists, he painted with Raymond Jonson. He frequented both the New Canton Cafe on San Fransisco Street and the Plaza Cafe with the Santa Fe artist group Los Cinco Pintores. His work has been exhibited worldwide, in the Corcoran Gallery in Washington, D.C., with the Paris World's Fair American Group of 1940 in Chicago; Ketchum, Idaho, and La Jolla, California. A 1996 exhibit introduced adventurous abstract acrylics on paper. "Architecture is discipline—painting is freedom. I need both," he explains his accomplishments.[*]

As the founder and chairman of the Northern New Mexico Civil Liberties Union and a member of the executive boards of St. Vincent Hospital, Santa Fe Legal Aid, and the Old Santa Fe Association, and as architect for the Santa Fe Housing Authority, William has changed the look, the feel, and the thinking of his community.

Never one to shrink from a new challenge or experience, in 1980 he ran Democratic Congressman Bill Richardson's first election campaign.

The author of three books on adobe construction, including *La Casa Adobe* and *Casa del Sol)* William modestly maintains, "My main asset has always been my curiosity."[**]

---

[*] William Clark, "Pioneer Upbringing Sparks Lumpkins' Designs, Paintings," *Albuquerque Journal*, October 13, 1987.
[**] Kathleen McCloud, "Fearless and Free, Lumpkins Show Spans Career," *New Mexican*, January19,1996.

"I didn't like the starving artist idea, so I went to architecture school. I always managed to paint, though; even during the war when there was 'hurry up and wait time' I did portraits."**
—*William Lumpkins*

Tommy Macaione

PAINTER, POLITICIAN, PONTIFICATOR

SOUTHBOUND MOTORISTS TRAVELING DOWN the Bajada on Interstate 25 toward Albuquerque may never have seen Tommy Macaione's masterpieces, but they knew how he felt about his work. "Messieurs Picasso, Monet, Van Gogh: Please step aside for Thomas S. Macaione, the new star of the world firmament. Let him bask in the light of world fame," the billboard proclaimed.

"El Diferente," and "Macaroni," as Tommy came to be known, arrived in Santa Fe in 1952. "It was Randall Davey's art school pictured in *Life* magazine and the great adobe haciendas . . . that attracted me to Santa Fe," he recalled. "The art colony looked like it would be an ideal place to go and settle, and maybe have a secure art life. But it turned out that Mr. Randall Davey had established himself as a great teacher. He was earning a good living. I, as an upstart, young fellow, had to work menial jobs. It was an awful hard climate. I starved mercilessly, you might say."

He soon found himself painting in the company of many of Santa Fe's noted artists—Alfred Morang, Randall Davey, Fremont Ellis, Gustave Baumann, and Will Shuster.

Born to Sicilian immigrants Maria and Joseph Macaione in New London, Connecticut, in 1907, Tommy spent his early childhood in Italy, when his homesick mother returned to Sicily with her four children. When World War I broke out, they were unable to return to the United States. Joseph was onboard a ship sailing to Palermo in 1918 when he contracted influenza and died.

Determined to study art when he returned to New London at age fifteen, Tommy worked briefly with private teachers. After serving as a soldier in World War II, he attended the Rhode Island School of Design and Art Students League in New York on the G.I.Bill. Tommy worked in New London as a barber and "starving artist" for twenty-five years. Then he headed west.

By 1961 he had established himself as a City Different persona. "Come With Me," Tommy beckoned as he posed with his dog, Windy, at landmarks throughout Santa Fe for a Ewen Enterprise publication, *A Different Guide to the City Different.* From then on many Santa Fe tourist publications included a photo of Tommy painting at one of his favorite spots.

He fashioned himself "an artist, philosopher, statesman, mortal prophet, and searcher of the truth in life."* He could be found most days painting and pontificating. In 1988, he delved into politics, announcing his candidacy for president on his "Mutual Happiness Society" platform.

Tommy never married. "A woman needs love and security. I can't provide the security." He was a great lover of animals.

Tommy celebrated his eightieth birthday with an exhibition of his paintings at the Museum of Fine Arts. Tommy's "works are passionate expressions of the subjects he paints," wrote then-museum curator Sandra D'Emilio. "Santa Fe's winding streets, adobe houses, flower-filled gardens, and flaming, golden fall aspens in Hyde Park, under Macaione's hand, become vibrant, colorful, expressive works which reflect the joy and reverence that Macaione has for all living things."

---

* From an article by Sally Eauclaire, *Southwest Profile* (February/March/April 1993).

Tim French & Alison French

"I made a vow
that I would ded-
icate my life to
painting God's
creation, in
praise of God
and his creation,
nature."

—*Tommy Macaione*

Dorothy McKibbin

"GATEKEEPER" OF LOS ALAMOS

As scientists from all over the free world poured into New Mexico in 1943 to work on the Manhattan Project, each and every one of them passed through the office, at 109 Palace Avenue, of Dorothy McKibbin. Traveling under assumed names, weary, bewildered, often with no idea where they were headed, they were grateful for her welcome and the yellow map, and the reassuring words, "Only thirty-five miles to go." With an exquisite combination of tact, intelligence, loyalty, hospitality, humor and motherly warmth, she served as "gatekeeper to Los Alamos." Throughout her life she maintained many close friendships with those she helped orient "to the Hill." More than twenty Los Alamos couples were married in her house on Old Santa Fe Trail.

Born in Kansas City, Missouri, in 1897, Dorothy graduated from Smith College in 1919 and later married Joseph C. McKibbin. Following his death in 1931 she moved to Santa Fe, where she worked for the Laboratory of Anthropology from 1943 until her retirement in 1963.

During wartime, security was so tight that Santa Feans referred to Los Alamos as a submarine base or the place where submarine windshield wipers were made. According to another cover, it was a camp for pregnant WACs. When a Santa Fean encountered a Hill resident and asked where he was from, the answer was inevitably a terse "Box 1663." Dorothy recalled how the word *physicist* was taboo.

"If there was no stranger around and I was feeling very wicked, I would glance in all directions, examine the empty air, raise an eyebrow, and whisper tensely, blowing through my teeth like a supressed wind instrument, 'Are you a phhh ht?'"

As a combination reception desk, information center, and travel bureau, Dorothy's office was a hub of life and emotion. She recalled: "109 East Palace was an information center, not too accurate, but always willing, for inquiries on how and where to get items ranging from horses to hair ribbons. Babies were parked here. Dogs were tied outside. Our trucks delivered baggage, express, and freight to the Hill and even special orders of flowers, hot rolls, baby cribs, and pumpernickel."

Many WACS and soldiers, who had been told they were being sent overseas, did not understand why they had landed in New Mexico. Dorothy comforted them when they were at their lowest ebb. She also served as a personnel director, interviewing the many people who applied for jobs on the Hill.

"When we were employed, we were told to ask no questions, and we didn't—much. We worked with pride. We sensed the excitement and suspense of the project, for the intensity of the people coming through the office was contagious. Working at 109 was more than just a job. It was an exciting experience."

---

* From *Standing By and Making Do: Women of Wartime Los Alamos,* edited by Jane S. Wilson and Charlotte Serber (Los Alamos, N.M.: Los Alamos Historical Society, 1988).

Allen L. Jennings

"Our office served as the entrance to one of the most significant undertakings of the war or, indeed, of the twentieth century."*

—*Dorothy McKibbin*

Virginia Mackie

A PROFOUND LOVE OF MUSIC

FROM HER EARLIEST YEARS, THE PIANO was part of Virginia Mackie's life. Taught to play at age three by her mother, at age ninety-four she was still practicing every day. Not only a pianist, Virginia also played the harpsichord, the Indian flute, and the recorder, as well as being a teacher of great influence.

"I've taught all my life," said the Kansas native. Through the years she taught over one thousand students. At the Conservatory of Music at the University of Missouri in Kansas City, Virginia taught piano, music theory, and ear training for twenty-five years. During this time she also accompanied dance groups, directed two choruses, played chamber music, and performed as a soloist, often with the local symphony. In addition, she taught at the University of Arizona and at the Yale School of Music for eighteen years. John Crosby, founder of the Santa Fe Opera, was one of her Yale students.

Her own distinguished training included a bachelor's degree in piano from Wellesley College, where she earned her Phi Beta Kappa key, a master's degree from Columbia University, studies in London, and training in France with the renowned instructor Nadia Boulanger. Virginia was one of only two of Boulanger's students to receive a degree in music theory pedagogy.

Virginia was grateful she first learned to play by ear and didn't read music until age five. Starting with church hymns, she found she could play "Christmas carols in any hand, any key."

The great classic composers were her favorites. Bach she found "so profound that you feel like you are looking into all the worlds that have been or ever will be." Of the challenges in facing the complex rhythms of classical music, she said, "You somehow or other have to rise to meet it." Regarding the effect of playing piano on human consciousness, she remarked, "You are always trying to approach the depths of your understanding through your hands."[*]

As part of her life's work, Virginia analyzed all the solo piano compositions of her favorite composer Franz Joseph Haydn, reviewing all the different editions of his sixty-two sonatas.[*]

Virginia first came to Santa Fe and stayed at Bishop's Lodge in the 1940s. She did not move to the city until the mid-1970s, following the death of her husband, a banker turned architect. When asked how she found living alone, she said, "I don't feel as if I am by myself. I feel as if I'm with Bach, Beethoven, Brahms, Mozart, and my boyfriend, Haydn."

---

[*] Craig Smith, "She's Been Making the Piano Sing for 80 Years: Virginia Mackie," *New Mexican*, n.d.

"A piano is not a singing instrument like a voice or a flute. You have to make it sing."*

—*Virginia Mackie*

Tona & Elias Maes

LEADERS OF THE GRAND MARCH

ONE OF SANTA FE'S MOST BELOVED COUPLES, Tona and Elias Maes lived a traditional way of life that has just about faded from the streets and the plaza into memory. Raising thirteen children—ten girls and three boys—in a small, century-old adobe house inherited from Elias's grandmother, they lived a life close to their Agua Fria community and their church, Our Lady of Guadalupe. Elias was also a prominent member of La Union Protectiva, a burial society. The couple lent spirit to weddings and fiestas around town. Skilful dancers, they were often called on to lead grand marches at wedding celebrations.

A plasterer by trade, Elias, born in 1904, made his own mortar and worked in the old style of lathe and plaster, tending to many of Santa Fe's historic homes and buildings. He remained in this profession over sixty years. "My first trade was a baker," he recalled, "and then I joined the National Guard and cooked there for eight years. That's my life. I did all kinds of work." In 1968, he retired from the Museum of New Mexico, where he worked as a guard. In wartime he worked at Los Alamos National Laboratory, as a carpenter, plasterer, guard, and cook. "I try to do everything," he told us.

In his youth, Elias was a professional boxer. Later he gained quite a reputation as a musician. For thirty years he played bass drum in a brass band that gave regular concerts on the gazebo that once stood at the center of the plaza. "I like to beat," he explained. He also sang for the Conquistadores, a band that played at Fiesta de Santa Fe, in La Fonda Hotel, and he was proud of the fact that his voice could carry great distances. He would use a megaphone, but never a microphone.

Tona lived simply, by the loving routines shaped by home, family, and church. She said: "I do housework, I like to embroider, and I do a lot of baking." She was well known for her elaborate embroidery, and she also worked as a cook and housekeeper for many of the town's most prominent families. With her husband, she enjoyed polkas and leading wedding marches, "sometimes two weddings in one day."

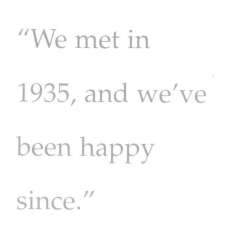

"We met in 1935, and we've been happy since."

—Elias Maes

John Manley

INFLUENCING THE COURSE OF HISTORY

"Y OU MAY ASK HOW A SCIENTIST who helped build the bomb can claim to be working for peace. The answer is simple. We were at war at the time, and I was working for peace in my way. Now that the war is over and we face another kind of nuclear threat, I've been working for peace in another way,"* said John Manley.

Handpicked by J. Robert Oppenheimer to coordinate the experimental aspects of atomic weapons development, John was "very doubtful about it, but finally agreed to do it on a trial basis." On April 4, 1943, John cautiously made his way up the primitive road to Los Alamos, carrying the fragile tube of a Cockroft-Walton accelerator in the back of a pickup. His initial tasks were to oversee the construction of laboratory buildings he had approved from Chicago "without having any knowledge of the terrain," and to install the accelerator.

"I didn't even know there was such a profession when I was in high school," he said, when asked why he became a physicist. "I went into electrical engineering. After a couple of years I found engineering was far too much cookbook stuff—learning how things were made but not why. My interest was in why."

Born to Benjamin and Effie Manley in 1907, John grew up an only child in Harvard, Illinois. "My family never had very much money," he recalled. "My father painfully worked his way through law school." John completed grade school and high school in Harvard, and earned a state fellowship at the University of Illinois.

John graduated in 1929 and accepted a tutoring job in Vienna for the winter. He returned to a fellowship at Westinghouse and received a doctorate in physics from the University of Michigan in 1934.

John met Kathleen Baird in New York when both were teaching at Columbia University. They married in 1935 and became parents to two daughters, Kathleen and Kim.

Immediately after Pearl Harbor was bombed, John received a phone call from physicist Leo Szilard, asking him to come and work on a special project—the Manhattan Project. The Manleys moved to Chicago in January 1942.

John worked as a nuclear physicist in Los Alamos from 1943 to 1946 and served as the technical associate director of the laboratory from 1947 to 1951. He resigned his position to become head of the physics department at the University of Washington in Seattle "because he did not want to work on the hydrogen bomb," said Kathleen. He returned to Los Alamos in 1957 "to do pure research and considered the lab to be the finest place to do this work."

John was involved in the negotiations that led to the creation of the Atomic Energy Commission and served as executive secretary of the Atomic Energy Commission's General Advisory Committee. The right-hand man of the United States ambassador to the Geneva talks on atomic energy, he played a major role in international atomic energy activities.

As he grew older, John became more involved in peace work, and lectured about the threat of nuclear war. He enrolled in a Soviet policy class in 1987 "because he wanted to analyze the situation in which we found ourselves throughout the Cold War," said Kathleen. "His ability to probe underlying causes and their inevitable results was fundamental throughout his life."

---

*From an article by Robert Storey, *New Mexican*, March 2, 1987.

"When I read in the *New Mexican* that I was called a physicist and a peace activist, I didn't like it. Then I realized that is what I have been."*

—*John Manley*

Peach Mayer

THE FIRST LADY OF OPERA

PHILANTHROPIST, ARTS PATRON, AND POLITICAL ACTIVIST, Katherine Mayer acquired the name Peach as a child when her family doctor insisted that Katherine had "cheeks like a peach."

Peach was born in 1905 to George and Berta Van Stone. Her father came to Santa Fe in 1896, seeking a climate that would help him recover from a pulmonary ailment.

When Peach and her brother, Tom, were small children, the Van Stones moved to Estancia, New Mexico, where her father owned a store and raised sheep. Music highlighted the family's evenings; George played the violin, and Berta the piano. The Van Stones returned to Santa Fe in 1912, the year New Mexico became a state, when George was elected state corporation commissioner. George died in 1914. Berta taught piano lessons and worked as curator of the Museum of Fine Arts to support her children.

While in high school Peach played a two-barrel organ at the Paris Theatre to earn money for college. She played basketball, was a cheerleader, sang in the glee club, and was a member of the drama club. When a South American company came to Santa Fe to perform *Rigoletto* in the former Elks Theatre, Peach became an opera aficionado. She served as Santa Fe Opera Board president for many years.

Seventeen-year-old Peach graduated from Santa Fe High School in 1922 and began teaching school in Cerrillos. She then studied for a year in Boston at Miss Wheelock's Kindergarten School, and received a scholarship to Colorado College in Colorado Springs, where she was elected president of the junior class at a time when women weren't considered presidential material. Peach graduated summa cum laude and returned to Santa Fe to teach at the Brownmoor School for Girls.

In 1934, Peach accepted a position with the New Mexico Department of Public Welfare. A drought and the Depression had brought hard times, and she received $18 per week as assistant supervisor of the Santa Fe County Emergency Relief.

She married Walter Mayer, a rancher and cattleman, in 1936. The newlyweds lived in Estancia, where Walter developed deep-well irrigation in the Estancia Valley. They also lived in Santa Fe in the home her parents had purchased in 1915. Peach and Walter became the parents of two sons, James and Tom.

Peach helped to found the Maternal Health Center in 1937, an action that resulted in a scolding from the pulpit. The clergy was opposed to an organization that provided contraception and birth control information. Undaunted, Peach served four terms as president of the board.

As a political activist, Peach, along with Robert O. Anderson, served twice as co-chairman of New Mexico's Republican campaign to elect Dwight Eisenhower president. She refused to support Richard Nixon, when he wouldn't give her his written promise to end the war in Vietnam. Peach was a four-time delegate to the Republican National Convention.

As a philanthropist and arts patron, Peach served on the board of the Museum of New Mexico for eighteen years, working diligently to develop rapport between the museum and the Legislature.

"First you have to have the right plan, then pick the right people to carry it out. Give them the authority and the responsibility to act, cheer them on, thank them, and leave them alone."

—*Peach Mayer,*
reflecting on her work
as head of organizations

Faith Meem

THE SPIRIT OF CIVILITY

FAITH MEEM'S INTEREST IN CONSTRUCTION CAME NATURALLY. Her father's "first love was construction—bricks and mortar. He invented some of the first modular houses," says Faith's daughter, Nancy Meem Wirth.

Born in 1902 to Faith Gregg Bemis and Albert Farwell Bemis, Faith grew up in the Boston suburb of Chestnut Hill. One of seven children, Faith and her father enjoyed doing construction projects together. Faith attended Vassar for a couple of years, but when she became unhappy, her father encouraged her to study art in France.

On her return, Faith wanted to study architecture. Women weren't admitted to MIT or Harvard in the 1920's. The two schools had created the Cambridge School of Design for women who wanted to study architecture and landscape design. Faith received her degree from this school in the late 1920s. Afterwards, she remodeled a house in Washington, D.C., and worked briefly in New York, "but it was during the Depression and jobs were scarce," Nancy said.

The man Faith would marry, architect John Gaw Meem, contracted tuberculosis and came to Santa Fe for his health in the early 1920s. He was establishing himself in his profession. and one of his best clients was a woman from Colorado Springs named Alice Bemis Taylor. Alice hired John to build the Colorado Springs Fine Arts Center.

She also asked him to hire her niece, Faith, as a draftsman in his office. John agreed, and Faith Bemis headed to Santa Fe. The only one of her siblings to go West, Faith felt New Mexico was like "being close to the sea because she could see the horizon," Nancy told us. "She became attuned and identified closely with the Southwest."

Faith and John were married in 1933. The couple lived in his office for a while and then bought property on Old Pecos Road, now Old Santa Fe Trail. "Together, they designed and built the split level part of the house in 1938," said Nancy, who now lives in the home. "I was born in 1937. My parents had a housewarming and christening for my first birthday when the house was completed."

Her husband's architectural career was burgeoning, and Faith gave John her total support as he designed the Cristo Rey Church, thirty-five buildings on the University of New Mexico campus, including the Zimmerman Library, as well as a number of homes in Santa Fe and Albuquerque. Meanwhile, Faith maintained an active interest in landscape design. She designed the gardens for her home and belonged to the Santa Fe Garden Club.

During World War II the Meems took in four sisters from England. "They lived with us for four years," and Faith and John were "consumed with the raising of five girls," said Nancy.

Faith also supported civic causes. Inspired by Margaret Sanger's work, Faith helped to establish the Maternal Health Center in Santa Fe. Faith and John were also enthusiastic backers of St. John's College. They donated land to the college, and Faith served on the college's Board of Directors. She was dedicated to the Episcopal Church of the Holy Faith, and, as a member of the Historic Santa Fe Foundation and the Old Santa Fe Association, she also worked to preserve traditional Santa Fe.

"Whatever you do, do it with your whole heart."   —*Faith Meem*

Sensei Nakazono

NATURAL HEALING PRACTITIONER

ONE OF SANTA FE'S AND THE COUNTRY'S first practitioners of non-Western medicine, Sensei Nakazono had a seemingly miraculous power to banish pain. He studied and taught acupuncture all his life. He studied macrobiotics with its originator, George Ohsawa, and encouraged his students to open natural food stores, now a local fixture. His therapies were grounded in a deep philosophy of life and human possibilities.

He came from a farm family in Southern Japan. His mother was a midwife who knew nutrition, herbs and massage and guided her son's early interest in healing arts. Coming of age in pre-World War II Japan, Sensei Nakazono was a rebel, in trouble with teachers for asking hard questions, like What is the meaning of one plus one equals two? "Unconsciously, I was asking for my freedom," he explained.

Judo was the focus of his youth. He earned his black belt at age fifteen. He learned bonesetting as part of the judo discipline. Acupuncture he resisted at first; it was not taken seriously in 1930s Japan. One night he came to the dojo with a bad toothache. His teacher took out the box of golden needles, and stuck one right into the aching nerve, twice. Within minutes of the initial shock,the pain subsided to a quite bearable vibration. From then on Sensei would spend his life studying acupuncture, first as an apprentice to Dr. Juzo Motoyama and later on, according to his own lights.

In postwar Europe he built a huge following of aikido students but didn't hesitate to leave for the US where, he felt, people were receptive to change. Camping at Hyde State Park, in the summer of 1970, he woke before daylight and heard a voice command, "You open your center here." He'd heard that confident voice before, as a soldier facing death in southern Manchuria during the war. It was a voice "you didn't argue with." In 1972 he returned to Santa Fe and opened a dojo on Alto Street, offering martial arts and acupuncture. His son Katuharu has kept up the practise.

The Kototama principle is the source of life energy that creates our human capacities, the five physical senses on the one hand, the spiritual capacity — imagination, intuition, the artistic sense — on the other. This ancient Japanese teaching is both doctrine and method, somewhat like mantric Yoga, in its use of spiritual vibrations produced by intoning "primal sounds." Sensei's study of the Kototama transformed his practise of acupuncture and his approach to diagnosis. He published many books on the subject. He didn't practise medicine, he said, but Kototama Life Therapy.

"He had a lot of love for people and his patients," daughter-in-law Sharon recalls. "He believed in giving people the tools to wake up, and that we knew at one time what we should be eating and how we should be living, with our natural rhythms in tune with natural cycles. We still have all this wisdom inside us and the way to save ourselves as human beings, with no need of laws or separate countries, is to get back to our own judgment."

"We're all dying from the time we're born."

—*Sensei Nakazono's*
reply to a sick man's question, "Am I dying?"

Rose Naranjo

POTTER AND MATRIARCH

WIDELY KNOWN AS A POTTER, her work treasured, collected, and honored, it is the traditions of pueblo and family that define the life of Santa Clara potter Rose Naranjo. The matriarch of a renowned family of artists, she raised ten children, eight of them born to her, and taught them all pottery making "so they could make a living." Rose saw to it that all her children, in a family that includes noted artists Michael Naranjo, Teresita Naranjo, Rina Swentzell, Jody Folwell, and Nora Naranjo-Morse, went to college. "I didn't have education," she said, "but I knew in the future they would need education. Every one of them got their college degree."

Pottery links the Naranjos to the world outside the pueblo; it also binds the generations together.

Born in 1917, Rose began working in clay in her teens. "Through the years, experience makes you good," she said. Raised by her grandmother Lupita, a midwife and medicine woman, Rose did not find out until her grandmother's death, when Rose was thirteen, that Lupita was not her mother. "Growing up was hard in those days," Rose remembered, "because we were so poor. She was the midwife, so when she went out to deliver a baby, we'd get food in exchange."

At eighteen Rose married Michael Naranjo, a Southern Baptist minister. They lived in Taos for twenty-seven years, and Rose did missionary work alongside her husband, throughout the Southwest. They had been married fifty-nine years when he died in 1994. Raising her family kept Rose busy. "In my day, the pueblo is children," she said. "And housework." At last count, she had thirty-four grandchildren. "I have lots of them. I don't count them anymore." And at age eighty, Rose was still making her extraordinary pots, "when I need to pay bills."

Rose's spiritual link to the pottery is very strong. With "good intention," her pots become an expression of her spirit, their making divinely guided from the digging of the clay to the firing, which she calls the "Judgment Day."

In her house at Santa Clara, Rose cooks on a woodstove and watches the ceremonial dances. "I sometimes sit here and look out the window, and I can see all the beauty of the old people that will be walking around." She continues to bake bread in her *horno* (outdoor oven), just as she continues to "bake" her potteries.

"Traditions are important to me, because I grew up with my grandmother and that's all we know, tradition. It's good. And it means a lot to me. The community means a lot to me. This is where I was born and raised."*

---

* From an article by Jim Jones, *Fort Worth Star Telegram*, n.d.
** Stephen Trimble, *Talking with the Clay: The Art of Pueblo Pottery* (Santa Fe, N.M.: School of American Research Press, 1987), 13.

"Clay is very selfish. It will form itself to what the clay wants to be."**

—*Rose Naranjo*

Lloyd Kiva New

TURNING TRADITIONAL CRAFTS INTO NEW ART FORMS

"THE INSTITUTE OF AMERICAN INDIAN ARTS should do one simple thing," says Lloyd Kiva New. "It should add to its vision—its goals, its objectives—an obligation to help every student who goes there make a good living." He insists, "One word—*design*—needs to be added to the name. Indian artists have been designers forever. At present, the institute is to train fine artists. Just think what we could contribute if we launched a series of programs in the area of design. Ultimately, we would have a whole new set of Indian furniture designers, fabric designers, fashion designers."

Lloyd arrived in Santa Fe in 1961 to serve as "the institute's art director and set up the arts program," he said. He served as the institute's president from 1965 to 1978, and returned in 1988 to guide the school through its separation from Bureau of Indian Affairs administration.

Born the tenth child "to a full-blood Cherokee mother and a Scott/Irish father" in 1916, he lived on a farm in northeastern Oklahoma. "By the time I was born, my mother had been injured while working in the hog pen, and she couldn't lift me."

One of the first things that fascinated him was clay. "I assume that I made the typical things that a five year old would make, little farm animals," he said. "I remember doing some dishes and things of that kind. My mother would bake little things I made in the wood oven as she was preparing meals."

An older sister became Lloyd's "nursemaid." "I was about eight when she got married. My mother asked her to take me and raise me. I think she knew that I wasn't going to make it on the farm, particularly with my father not being sympathet-ic to things other than doing his job, which was to make a living for the family."

Lloyd attended school in an oil-rich suburb of Tulsa. "It was kind of a hellish period of being sort of closed in by life," he said. "I was kind of a loner." He was valedictorian of his high school class in 1933 and then enrolled at Oklahoma A & M. Unable to find art classes, he decided to leave college. "Well, if you can't get what you want at that school, why don't you go somewhere else, where you can?" his mother had wisely asked.

"When I went to the Art Institute of Chicago in the 1930s, I think there were only fifteen Indians in higher education, and we were all under Bureau of Indian Affairs sponsorship," Lloyd recalled. "It was there I first discovered classic Indian cultures."

After serving as a commissioned navy officer in the Pacific in World War II, he settled in Scottsdale, Arizona, and became known for his "kiva bags," a line of women's handbags that were market-ed by stores such as Neiman Marcus and Elizabeth Arden. Other Indian artisans joined him, and the Lloyd Kiva Crafts Center they established gained an international reputation. During this period, he was "devoted to the problem: can Indian craftsmen pro-duce contemporary craft items for general use, enabling the craftsmen to earn a living, pursuing their crafts in a general society?" He characterized the whole problem of the deterioration of Indian art "as the beaded rabbit's foot syndrome." Although he had achieved financial success, Lloyd took the summers to teach because he was "still concerned that Bureau of Indian Affairs teachers weren't teaching art."

"I had characterized the deterioration of Indian art as the beaded rabbit's foot syndrome."

—*Lloyd Kiva New*

Beaumont Newhall

AUTHOR OF THE HISTORY OF PHOTOGRAPHY

PHOTOGRAPHIC HISTORIAN Beaumont Newhall's earliest memory is set in a darkroom. "I was standing beside my mother in her darkroom while she was developing plates," he recalled. "I thought it was magic that made a picture on a piece of glass."

Born in 1908, Beaumont spent his childhood in Lynn, Massachusetts, before going off to Andover Academy and Harvard. Although he had a desire to study film and photography, he settled on art history as the most closely-related subject Harvard offered at the time. "I loved it," he said, and even though he came of age during the Depression, in 1931 his teacher and mentor Paul J. Sachs helped him find a job at the Pennsylvania Museum of Art in Philadelphia. Following studies in Paris, in 1935 he became librarian at the then seven-year-old Museum of Modern Art in New York City. There, in 1937, he curated MOMA's first photography show, an overview of the art form.

As historian, curator, writer, teacher, and photographer, Beaumont went on to articulate the value of photography as a fine art. Largely through his critical appreciation of photography, the medium gained acceptance as an art form. He was to author some six hundred books, articles, and museum catalogs, many in collaboration with his wife, Nancy. His classic *History of Photography, 1839 to the Present* remains the most widely-used text in its field.

During World War II, Beaumont worked in photoreconnaissance in Egypt, Italy, and North Africa, then went on to become curator of Kodak's photography museum, George Eastman House, in Rochester, New York. In addition to curating numerous shows for the museum in Rochester, Beaumont assured his reputation as a fine cook with a weekly newspaper column, the "Epicure Corner," for seven years; and by cooking lunch for noted chef James Beard. (He served *choucroute garni* and Beard took three helpings.)

Beaumont came to New Mexico in the early 1970s to teach at the University of New Mexico and moved to Santa Fe in 1975. A mentor to many of the city's younger writers and photographers, his generosity, gentleness, and dedication were well known. He took great pride in the publications his students produced. He began exhibiting his own photography. as well. In 1985, he received a MacArthur Foundation Fellowship, the so-called "genius grant."

In the Santa Fe home designed by his second wife, Christi, Beaumont enjoyed gardening and playing with his "pack" of a half-dozen dogs. His autobiography, *Focus: Memoirs of a Life in Photography,* is a chronicle of photography in this century, featuring all the artists, museum and gallery people, and patrons with whom he shared and inspired a great excitement.

"Photography has been to me what a journal has been to a writer, a record of things seen and experienced, moments in the flow of time, documents of significance to me, experiments in 'seeing.'"   —*Beaumont Newhall*

Ben Ortega

SEARCHING FOR LEÑA

"MY FAVORITE IS SAINT FRANCIS because it was my first piece that got sold," Ben Ortega says of his woodcarvings. "I tell everybody that Saint Francis didn't want me to go to California."

His carvings are in collections world-wide, yet Ben never planned to be an artist. "I used to sit in the kitchen and make little faces. I made two Indians—small pieces—and then I carved a little Saint Francis. Mrs. Myrtle Stedman [the artist and builder] saw my carvings. She loved them so much I gave her the Indians. I used to work for her, picking apples and peaches when I was a little boy."

Born in Tesuque, New Mexico, in 1923 to Isador and Agnes Ortega, Ben and his two brothers and sister were raised by an aunt and uncle. "My mother died in an automobile accident when I was two," he said. "My father died when I was six."

He grew up poor, but blessed with love, and had to quit school in the eighth grade. At eighteen, he "went to the war." Serving with the 240th Combat Engineers, he went "overseas—straight from San Francisco to New Guinea. It took twenty-eight days to get there." He was in Dutch New Guinea and then in the Philippines "ready to go to China or the mainland of Japan when the war ended." He "returned home five or six months after the bomb was dropped."

Back in Tesuque, he enrolled in school. "The only time I have been out of Tesuque was those three years, and I was always thinking about the beautiful Tesuque Valley that I love so much," he said. He took two years of cabinet making and machine shop in Santa Fe. He planned to go to California with classmates to find work. "While I was waiting to go, I decided I was going to carve something just to pass the time," he said, "so I . . . carved a little Saint Francis and a little Madonna."

Asked if he had anything he could contribute to a benefit sale for the Santa Fe Opera, Ben donated his two carvings. They sold at once. "That evening, there was somebody knocking on my door. This lady from New York asked, 'Are you Ben Ortega, the artist?' I said, 'No, I'm just Ben Ortega.' She asked me to make a Saint Francis. When she came back, her sister wanted a Madonna. A friend wanted a crucifix."

Six months later, Ben had a one-man show at the Museum of Fine Arts in Santa Fe. His thirty-five pieces sold in forty-five minutes, and Ben stayed home in his beloved Tesuque Valley.

Ben met Isabelle Lovato in Santa Fe. "We got married in 1948 and have five sons and five daughters—all professional woodcarvers. I taught them to carve when they were small." Ben is grateful for family. "I pray to God and give thanks to God for keeping my family together. We're not rich, but God has blessed us with a good family. What more can a guy ask for?"

Ben and Isabelle traveled to Washington, D.C., in 1976 to take part in the Bicentennial Festival of American Folklore at the Smithsonian Institution. "Isabelle demonstrated Mexican and Spanish cooking, and I demonstrated woodcarving," he said.

When the weather is nice, Ben and Isabelle get in their truck and drive hundreds of miles in northern New Mexico, searching for leña (wood). "I know what I like," he said. So do his many admirers.

"Sometimes I see faces in the wood."   —*Ben Ortega*

Alfonso Ortiz

ACTIVIST ANTHROPOLOGIST

Traditional teachings of the Pueblo way of life guide cultural anthropologist Alfonso Ortiz in all his writing, teaching, and commitments to social service. Born in 1939 and raised at San Juan Pueblo, the MacArthur Fellow says: "I like to balance my life. I like to balance a life of service with the books, articles, and teaching."

His *New Perspectives on the Pueblos* and *The Tewa World* break new ground, giving outsiders an intimate understanding of Indian ways. Alfonso has also written extensively on American Indian myths, legends and tribal histories, and served as editor for the Smithsonian Institution's twenty-volume *Handbook of Native American Indians*. A distinguished scholar who has taught at Princeton, Berkeley, Rutgers, Colorado College, Claremont College, and the University of New Mexico (UNM), he remains close to his roots.

Alfonso remembers his youth at San Juan Pueblo during World War II as "very, very happy," although his family was poor. "I can't imagine any better way to grow up," he reflects. "I was raised by my culturally conservative grandparents. I was roused at 4 A.M. by my grandfather to go to the fields, to irrigate and transplant. During the hottest hours, the boys went swimming in the Rio Grande, then, it was back to the fields. It was a life of hard work, discipline, activity, and lots of fun."

As a student at UNM during the late 1950s and early 1960s, Alfonso chose a sociology major with a political science minor. He planned to attend law school. "Although there were no Indian lawyers, I was repelled when I got closer to the profession," he recalls. In a quandary about his future, he enrolled in a one-year master's degree program in Indian education at Arizona State University. There, he met his mentor, distinguished anthropologist Edward Dozier, who encouraged him to continue his studies outside the region, to avoid the label of provincialism. At the University of Chicago, Alfonso met people from all over the country and the world.

As an undergraduate, Alfonso took an active part in University of New Mexico campus politics. His public role has expanded with the years. A professor of anthropology at UNM, he is also a respected spokesperson for Indian concerns outside of academia. An environmental activist, he has been a vocal opponent of the proposed Jemez Mountains power line, that would threaten rare species of medicinal and ceremonial plants. He served as a consultant to the makers of the award winning documentary film, Surviving Columbus, a history of the Pueblos. He was president of the American Association on American Indian Affairs for fifteen years, and chairman of the National Advisory Council at the Newberry Library's Center for the History of American Indians. In Santa Fe he serves on the board of the Chamisa Foundation and with the City Arts Commission's Advisory Council.

A life of service, as "drummed into [him] by [his] grandparents" guides him in all his spheres of influence. "When I was growing up, the community looked after everyone," he says. "Those who brought in a good harvest would have to share with those who had a poor harvest. We were imbued with this idea: you look to where you can serve."

"The Pueblo way
is: you don't live
for yourself, you
live for others.
There's always
someone who
needs your help,
someone less
fortunate."

—*Alfonso Ortiz*

Hazel Parcells

HEALING PIONEER

BORN IN GLENWOOD SPRINGS, COLORADO, IN 1889, Hazel Parcells set out on her journey in self-healing more than seventy years ago. When Hazel went to see her doctor in 1931, she was told she was dying. For fifteen years, she had been given drugs for heart problems. Most of her right kidney had been destroyed, her lungs were hemorrhaging daily, her heart was enlarged, and she had advanced tuberculosis.

Doctors recommended that Hazel enter a sanitarium for three years. She chose to keep working at the beauty parlor she owned. A diet of milk and eggs was recommended. She didn't follow it. "I had a desire for something green," she recalled. She purchased spinach. "Suddenly, all I wanted was spinach. I ate that green spinach raw, cooked, hot and cold, for breakfast—for every meal."

Six months after Hazel had been declared a "medical reject," doctors couldn't explain her remarkable recovery. Her kidney was healing, and " . . . there wasn't even scar tissue in the lungs," she recalled. "I hadn't taken any medications. The heart condition had cleared up. At that time, no one knew anything about electrical energy in healing, and certainly nothing green as part of it. Spinach, at that point, was our commercial source of folic acid. No cell can be rejuvenated or rebuilt without it."

As her quest for wellness continued, Hazel became a doctor of naturopathy. She earned chiropractic certification, stud-ied homeopathy, and received a doctorate in comparative religions.

Hazel arrived in Albuquerque in 1968. She didn't advertise. She didn't solicit. She didn't distribute any information, yet many people sought her counsel.

"I don't care what your problem is, naturally there's a point of no return. When you reach that point, there's very little that can be done other than to make people comfortable," she explained. "And, at that point, usually you've been cut up—drugged—so that everything that you had that would help you is gone. . . . I'm not very interested in drugs.

"The function of the cell is all that we have to work with, and it can only function properly when it's in balance with its electrical magnetic energy. That is your life itself. Nothing can exist . . . outside its own environment and its own energy field," she said. "You don't have to kill anything. All you have to do is change the environment, and it is taken care of. All things live in their own environment."

Doctors don't know why things have happened "because they've never gone into it," Hazel maintained. "Do you know that the medical profession, outside of the invasion of drugs, their whole philosophy hasn't changed in one hundred years? Now we are coming into a new age—a new era—where our philosophy is going to change because necessity is going to make it change."

"I don't know of any physical reason that I should leave this planet anytime. I've learned how to live."   —*Hazel Parcells*

Polly Patraw

A GRAND CANYON LIFE

"It was my engagement present," Polly Patraw said of the Navajo rug displayed on the couch in the living room of her Santa Fe home. A painting of the Grand Canyon's North Rim hangs above the couch—a reminder of special times in Polly's life.

Polly was staying at the VT Dude Ranch in 1928 and collecting plants to study for her master's thesis, a "general ecological description of the Kaibob Plateau." Riding horseback, she had "a bedroll, a canteen of water, and a plant press." One day an invitation awaited her when she returned from the field. "I was invited to attend a dinner for the dedication of the Grand Canyon's North Rim Lodge. I dug in my trunk, got out a dress, and got myself down to the North Rim,"Polly said. "I ate dinner with Stephen Mather, the founder and first director of the National Park Service; Mormon Church President Heber J. Grant; and Carl Grey, president of the Union Pacific Railroad."

Born in 1904 in Longmont, Colorado, Polly was the sixth child of Paul and Ariet Mead. "My father and mother founded the town of Mead in 1906," she said. "They were very religious, straight-laced, and stipulated that no alcoholic beverages be sold in Mead. We later moved to Berthoud. I attended a little one-room schoolhouse. I loved working on the farm, and I loved the flowers—fields of daisies. I used to ride a bicycle three miles to take my music lessons. I loved the piano." Her father had a cattle ranch near Lyons, where Polly spent her summers in the mountains. Her mother was a teacher.

Around 1920 Polly traveled by train to Chicago to live with an aunt and uncle while she attended the University of Chicago High School. There, she became friends with Stephen Mather's daughter, Bertha. Polly graduated from "U High" in 1924.

Later, she received her bachelor's and master's degrees in botany from the University of Chicago. "For my graduation present, my aunt offered me a trip to Europe, or I could go to the Grand Canyon and work on my master's. I've never been to Europe," Polly told us, without regret.

She applied for a job at the Grand Canyon in 1930 and became one of the first women ranger naturalists in the National Park Service. "In 1930, they didn't hire women," she recollected. Preston "Pat" Patraw was the assistant superintendent. In March 1931, Pat took Polly "for a ride along the rim to see the scenery," and they got engaged. They were married in Phoenix in May.

"Pat wanted me to be home, and in those days you said, 'Yes, dear,'" Polly remarked. Pat was superintendent of Zion and Bryce National Parks when their children were born—in California—because there were no doctors nearby in the wilds of Utah. "The Park Service always wants things to fit with the scenery, so I was a good Park Service wife," said Polly. "My children had red hair to match the rocks." The Patraws moved to Santa Fe in 1947.

Fellow botanists praise Polly as "one of those women who do a great deal quietly, and don't ask for recognition." They remember it was Polly who did the plant inventory at Pecos National Monument. Her field guide, *Flowers of the Southwestern Mesas* (1951) pioneered the genre in this region. Its enduring popularity—55,000 copies sold—spurred the publisher, Southwest Monuments Association, to follow up with an entire series.

"I was one of
the first women
ranger naturalists
in the Park
Service."
—*Polly Patraw*

Rheua Pearce

LIVING THE CREATIVE PROCESS

WELL INTO HER NINETIES, Rheua Pearce held weekly informal dinner meetings at her home, the oldest house in Las Vegas, New Mexico. Her eyesight and hearing were failing, but no matter. The purpose of these confabs was to encourage her guests to network. She invited professors, city officials, and representatives from the Chamber of Commerce and the United World College to discuss topics ranging from intergenerational communication to world peace.

Stacks of folding chairs were kept in each room so that Rheua could hold several meetings at the same time. "I believe strongly that whether you live in Las Vegas, New Mexico, or anywhere else, you occupy a spot of latitude and longitude,"* said Rheua.

Born in 1894 to a pioneer family in northern Indiana, she was raised by her grandfather from the age of four. It was from him that Rheua learned the importance of being herself as well as the value of helping others, she said. "He was interested in everybody. He had a deep understanding of people. . . . He'd take me to poor farms and ask me, 'What do you think about how people are being treated here?' . . . He believed in the significance and value of each individual."*

Rheua was eighteen when she was chosen by Jane Addams to work with Chicago's poor at Hull House. There she initiated a Meals on Wheels program and began a pilot study for the United States Public Health Service. She earned her bachelor's degree in 1917 from the University of Chicago, the school where social work had its beginnings.

In 1930, Rheua moved to Las Vegas to recover from tuberculosis. She was fifty when she joined the Women's Army Corps during World War II. After the war, Rheua traveled in the Balkans as a welfare officer doing relief work for the United Nations. She also visited nine European countries as a member of the Women's International Democratic Federation.

While teaching at a one-room school at Conchas Dam near Tucumcari, Rheua introduced her students and their parents to the concept of an ungraded classroom. She arranged the chairs in a circle instead of in rows, and she told the children and visiting parents, "Anyone who laughs at a person who doesn't know something is a stupid person. The person who says 'I don't know but I want to learn' is a wise person." Thirty years later, Rheua invited her former students and their families to a reunion. Forty people came. Some hadn't seen each other for thirty years. Tape recordings were made to document school memories and the classmates' present endeavors.

Upon being named a Living Treasure, Rheua remarked: "We are people for whom it is an art to be just folks. All of us have been good at just being ourselves."*

In a prayer she wrote, Rheua shared her philosophy of life: "Dear God, help me to keep it simple. Help me to make my goings out and my comings in purposeful. Help me to make the utterances of my mouth and the meditations of my heart significant that I may not babble. Help me to keep my motivation true, devoid of ego and pomposity. Help me to always realize that Thou art the source of all inspiration and creative ability. Dear God, help me to keep it simple."

---

*From an article by Jim Terr, *New Mexican*, October 13, 1986.

"Any child that is born is occupying space on the globe, and that space is important . . . we need to do what is right here at hand for us to do."*

—*Rheua Pearce*

Mel Pfaelzer

SUPPORTER OF EDUCATION AND THE ARTS

WHEN MEL PFAELZER DECIDED TO GO into the ink business, he broke with family tradition. "His father was in the meat business for sixty years with Swift and Company. All the Pfaelzer men were in the meat business," says his wife, Dicky Pfaelzer.

Born in Chicago in 1908 to Abe and Lily Pfaelzer, Mel was their only son. He had one sister, Beatrice. "He was the golden boy. His parents worshipped him," Dicky recalls.

His father was a horse person, and Mel's love of horses was immediate. "Mel showed at the International when he was six, at the Royal in Kansas City when he was eight, and he began showing for other people when he was eleven. His father was the only man in the Chicago stockyards who rode a horse English gaited. Everyone else rode quarter horses."

Mel attended a private school, the Harvard School for Boys. "He was always very involved in sports and with horses," Dicky said. "He was also a Golden Gloves boxer—fortunately, he gave that up."

Rita Weil was fourteen when she met her husband-to-be. Mel married Rita in 1932. "It took her five years to catch him," says Dicky. Mel and Rita had two daughters, Jill and Nancy. Rita died tragically of a brain aneurysm, in 1956.

Mel married Dicky, Rita's sister, in 1957. "I've known Mel all my life," she says. "We were together only thirty-one years. I wish it could have been longer."

Mel worked in the printing business from 1936 to 1975 and was president of Bowers Printing Ink Company in Chicago. He served on the board of the National Association of Printing Ink Manufacturers.

He was also a dog lover, and "started the first obedience class for dogs in Chicago".

When Mel sold his business in 1975, he and Dicky moved to Tesuque. Dicky first came to Santa Fe in 1934, "but we built a house that was finished in 1972." After moving to New Mexico, Dicky, who had worked for art galleries in Chicago, went to work for Elaine Horwitch. Coming to Santa Fe provided Mel the opportunity to "finally live with his horses." In Tesuque, he lived at the edge of the national forest. It was the first time that he could ride every day—except Monday, which was the horse's day off.

In Santa Fe, Mel served on the boards of the Wheelwright Museum and the Santa Fe Opera. He was a trustee at the College of Santa Fe, where he helped establish scholarship programs for students, and a memorial scholarship was funded in his name.

Mel loved prints, and donated his graphics collection to Northern Illinois University.

"He was a real supporter of the arts, and he helped many local artists by purchasing and donating their work," says artist Paul Pletka. "I had a one-man show at the Museum of Fine Arts in 1990. Mel was instrumental in making the arrangements for that show. If you ran into a situation that you couldn't quite grasp or needed help with, you called Mel. He understood life."

---

*From an article by Kay Bird, *New Mexican*, December 4, 1988.

Kathy, Rick & Liza Abeles

"He was a centaur. He looked like he was half man, half horse."*

—*Photographer*

Barbara Van Cleve

describing Mel Pfaelzer

Photography by Barbara Van Cleve

Maggie Phinney

VOLUNTEERISM AS A PROFESSION

Maggie Phinney celebrated America's Bicentennial in a big way. Living in London in the 1970s, she decided to give the British an unforgettable exhibit of American Indian art. From the teeming basement of the British Museum, came carvings Capt Cook acquired in the Pacific Northwest. From the Ashmolean at Oxford, came Powhatan's robes. From the Rheims Cathedral came wampum belts collected by early French missionaries. It took a committee of one hundred—under Maggie's leadership — five years to prepare this major show. "Sacred Circles: Two Thousand years of North American Indian Art" drew record crowds to London's Hayward Gallery. Only Matisse ever had a bigger turnout. And she did it all as a volunteer.

"The first time I remember doing volunteer work was at sixteen," she told us. "My parents taught me that if I could afford to volunteer—both financially and time wise —I had a responsbility to give back to the community."

Growing up in Kansas City, she looked to her mother "as the role model from whom I learned the importance of volunteerism. She helped start Planned Parenthood in Kansas City, was involved in parent-teacher associations and founded the tea room, now a renowned restaurant at Kansas City's Nelson Gallery."

Maggie spent childhood summers on her grandfather's ranch outside Raton. Her mother's father was born in 1842. After college "he traveled to Raton. He met an English doctor who encouraged him to buy land. He did so, and the property is still in the family after more than a hundred years."

She majored in art history at Smith College, and found work with the fine arts department at IBM in New York. During the Second World War, "working full time and volunteering at a hospital three or four nights a week," she recalls, "I got to the point where I was putting on rouge to hide the circles underneath my eyes." Her father came to visit, went home and "tattled" to Maggie's mother. She returned to a less strenuous life in Kansas City, still volunteering with the Junior League.

Working as an international sales rep for Braniff Airways, she met and married Bob Phinney. When Bob, by then Braniff's Vice President, was posted to London for sixteen years, Maggie immersed herself in Ango-American activities, as a volunteer.

While the US celebrated its Bicentennial, Maggie's brainchild, the American Indian art exhibit, was making British history. Docents—laypeople who serve as volunteer museum guides—were unknown in Britain, until an American colleague of Maggie's began training them for the Sacred Circles show. $50,000 in profits from the show, went into the newly created Sacred Circles Foundation. To date,Maggie reports, "approximately $50,000 has been given to various Indian organizations, while the principal remains untouched."

Bob and Maggie became Santa Feans in 1981. Maggie has been President of the board of Open Hands, vice president and chair of membership at the Wheelwright Museum, and an Old Santa Fe Association Board member. "I'm retired—to a point," she says. "I'm not going to be chairman of anything any more. But I'll always be available for spot jobs."

"Volunteerism is, to me, just a way of life. I don't know what I'd do if I didn't volunteer."

—Maggie Phinney

Edith Pierpont

PROTECTOR OF THE ENVIRONMENT

ALTHOUGH MANY PEOPLE RETIRE TO SANTA FE in pursuit of a life of leisure, for Edith Pierpont retirement welded her life-long interests and talents into a new public career. In New Mexico, at the age of sixty-one, she became a lobbyist for the environmental movement.

Born in Worcester, Massachusetts, in 1922 and raised with a deep appreciation for the nearby New England countryside, Edith was trained from an early age to observe and appreciate nature. Her physician father, a great nature lover, taught his children how to look at birds and flowers. "He taught by example about the things that grew around us," Edith recalled.

"As World War II came in, we grew a victory garden in the middle of the front lawn. During the 1940s, Father got interested in organic gardening, which we discussed at the dinner table."

Edith's education at Vassar College left her with "some strong role models for educated women" and a sense of "obligation and excitement about using whatever interests you for improving the world." Her visit to West Virginia coal mining towns and factories in the East gave her "a sense of what people were doing to the earth."

With her husband, John H. Pierpont, a public relations executive, Edith raised her own five children, in turn, with an awareness of nature. As she became more interested in politics, she shifted her focus from her children's school activities to work as a reporter on her local newspaper. She interviewed many political figures, followed political campaigns, and cov-

ered environmental issues for ten years. She also earned a master's degree from Columbia University Teachers College, and taught school.

After moving to Santa Fe Edith transferred her League of Women Voters membership here. Gradually, she began writing material on local environmental issues. Then "they took me to the Roundhouse and introduced me to people," she explained. "I began to get a feeling for lobbying and got into lobbying all the time." She became the State League's Natural Resource Chair, and educated herself and others on land use, water, hazardous waste, and nuclear waste issues. The real excitement came for her when she learned how to form networks with other like-minded people and organizations, and to experience the effectiveness of coalitions in the political process.

"The passage of the Solid Waste Act of 1990 was a great example of a coalition working," she points out. She was also involved in other key pieces of legislation, such as the New Mexico Mining Act of 1993.

She served many years on the board of the New Mexico Environmental Law Center, an organization which provides free legal services for the protection of New Mexico's environment.

Edith's optimism about what can be accomplished for the environment on the local level has remained strong. "There is a real movement to try to get all the different groups together," she says. "This is the most hopeful part." At age seventy-four, she remains an active lobbyist, as well as a highly respected consultant to state agencies on environmental issues.

"We must keep up the political pressure in order to prevent fur- ther environ- mental losses."

—*Edith Pierpont*

Pauline Pollock

PLAZA RETAILER

As SOME SHOW BUSINESS CHILDREN are said to be born in a trunk backstage, with performing in their blood, Pauline Pollock was practically born in a clothing shop, with a predestined love for fashion and retail.

Pauline was born in Hot Springs, Arkansas, in 1903. Her German-Jewish merchant parents brought their only child to Santa Fe as a tiny baby. In 1912, the year of statehood, they opened "the first style store in Santa Fe" on the plaza. Called the White House, it was the first store that didn't sell "wagon wheels and whips" along with clothing, according to Pauline. "We had everything: infants, children, preteen, juniors, and we used to have piece goods, too."

In those days all women's ready-to-wear stores were called either the White House or the Emporium; and all shoe stores were called the Guarantee. Later on, the plaza store was named the Guarantee, after the shoe division Pauline's husband ran. This business lasted for four generations.

Pauline has many vivid memories of Santa Fe in the early days of the century. "I remember when we used to go 'round the plaza in a hack, and the mud came up to the middle of the wheels. The first residential street was Palace Avenue, then Don Gaspar," where she lived for forty-five years. "You'd go down the street and you'd know the names of all the little children. But you don't anymore."

La Fonda Hotel was the center of social life then, the place to stay and meet people. Parties and get-togethers were frequent. "Every Saturday night you'd look for a light," she said. "That was a party—it was very social. El Nido was one of our first eating places."

Married at eighteen in the Alvarado Hotel in Albuquerque, she and her husband first lived in a small apartment on Alameda. "It was so little that for our wedding my parents gave us a bedroom suite, and it furnished the whole house." Pauline met her husband, Barnett W. Petchesky, who was also in the clothing business, while still at finishing school in Bethlehem, Pennsylvania. He joined the family business, working alongside her very active businesswoman mother, who sometimes stayed in New York on buying trips six weeks at a time.

Pauline and her husband also bought a hog ranch on the south side of town. "It was almost like homesteading," she said. "We used to get the best garbage from La Fonda."

Eventually, when her two children were almost grown, Pauline took an active part in the family business: buying, selling, and managing. Her activity continued well into her senior years and sustained her through the loss of two husbands. She was seventy-seven at the death of Emil Pollock, her second husband. "I wouldn't be a person to stay home and play bridge all day," she reasoned, "so I might as well be productive." She remained involved even though her son and daughter later handled the bulk of the business, while her grandson worked in the shoe department.

Although involved with a clothing store for many years, Pauline likes to say, "I haven't given up my whole life to business." Serving on the board of the Boys Club for over twenty years, active in the Women's Club and Library Association, Pauline enthusiastically supported community activities.

"Every season, it all looks so wonderful—like I've never seen any of it before."   —*Pauline Pollock*

Juan Quintana

GRATEFUL AMIDST ADVERSITY

A POSTER OF AUTHOR/LECTURER AND FRIEND Ram Dass hangs on the wall, a constant reminder that when Ram Dass is in town, he'll stop to visit. A *nicho* made by the loving hands of his *Mamacita* sits on a shelf. Music, his constant companion, plays softly.

Juan Quintana's home since 1990 has been his room at La Residencia, a facility he entered when his multiple sclerosis became so advanced that he required full-time care.

Born Juan Miguel Quintana in 1959 in Santa Fe, the middle child and first-born son of Conchita and Juan Quintana, Juan attended school at Salazar Elementary, De Vargas Junior High, and Santa Fe High School.

When President John Kennedy was assassinated, Conchita watched the news broadcasts and wept. "It happened in November during hunting season," she recalled. Several days before Kennedy was killed, the Quintana family had been discussing hunting season around the family dinner table. Juan was told that sometimes hunters think they see a deer and mistakenly shoot humans. As she sobbed for the President, little Juan put his arms around his mother and said, "Mom, don't cry. Maybe that man thought he was a deer."

Juan liked to help his mother with her tinwork; he did the curling for her. In 1968, nine-year-old Juan explored every corner of the Smithsonian Institution while his mother demonstrated the art of tinsmithing.

He grew interested in bicycles in his teen years and found a job at a bicycle shop. Although his father opposed the purchase, Juan saved $500 and bought himself a bicycle. He often rose early in the morning and rode to Tesuque or Glorieta.

Juan met his German wife, Dagmar Kupinski, in Roswell in 1978, while attending an anti-nuclear rally. The couple spent two years in Europe, and Juan became fluent in German. Their daughter, Bgorg, was born in 1980. Visits and letters from Bgorg, who lives in Washington, are a highlight of Juan's life, his mother said.

While building homes in Santa Fe, Juan learned to speak Spanish by conversing with three men from Mexico who worked on his crew. Since they spoke little English, he began to feel "a bit of my heritage." Juan had been building homes for about six years when his balance became poor and he began to feel fatigued. No longer able to do construction work, he went back to bicycle repair.

Diagnosed with multiple sclerosis, Juan, a self-described "virtual hermit," found that he needed help, so he created a wide network of family and friends. Friends took him to the Natural Cafe and fed him his evening meal. His brother devised grab bars so that Juan could get around his apartment. Cab drivers took Juan wherever he wished to go, but as his illness progressed his outings were no longer possible. Juan's friends now visit him at La Residencia.

The youngest person to be named a Living Treasure, Juan was honored at age twenty-nine. "I thank Divinity for all the people that surround me with so much loving care and help. I only hope that I am grateful enough," was his response.

McCune Charitable Foundation

"People hope to console him—to lift his spirits. But when they leave, Juan has lifted theirs."

—*Conchita Lopez describing her son, Juan Quintana*

Tony Reyna

SERVICE TO PUEBLO AND NATION

TWICE NAMED GOVERNOR OF TAOS PUEBLO, Tony Reyna has lived a life of service to his people, his community, and his country. While serving in the army during World War II, he spent three and a half years as a prisoner of war. Captured by the Japanese along with hundreds of other New Mexico soldiers in the Philippines, he was sent on the Bataan Death March. He was tortured and forced to bury hundreds of people, his best friend among them. "Determination kept me going," he remembers. "I had a family, a home to come back to," said Tony.

Born in 1915, Tony has pleasant memories of growing up at Taos Pueblo. "By the time we could carry a bucket, we were carrying water and wood for mother to cook. We would run home from school to water and feed the horses. We would ride into town bareback to get kerosene. Those were very enjoyable days. We thought it was very hard, but looking back, it was very worthwhile. We learned to work and to take responsibility." Educated at the Taos Pueblo Day School and the Santa Fe Indian School, Tony graduated from Santa Fe High School in 1936.

"It was so important, the care my father and mother gave us, their commitment to us—they said, 'Don't take. Give something back. That's the philosophy we live by.'"

Tony's accomplishments reflect that philosophy of his parents. He has been a police commissioner for the town of Taos, a member of the Taos School Board, a trustee of the Millicent Rogers Museum, a judge at Santa Fe Indian Market, and is a lifetime member of the Taos Pueblo Council.

As governor of Taos Pueblo, he took responsibility for the welfare of his people, including the protection of the resources of the pueblo such as water rights and ditches; the preservation of structures; and the construction of a health clinic. To prepare for this job, he first served as tribal secretary and lieutenant governor of the pueblo.

Tony raised four children. One daughter, Diane Reyna, is known for her work in television and as the director of the Peabody Award-winning video *Surviving Columbus,* about the history of the Pueblo Indians after contact with the Spanish. One son, John Anthony, teaches at the Contemporary Indian School in Rowe, New Mexico; another son, Phillip, is manager of the Tony Reyna Indian Shop at Taos Pueblo. His daughter Marie Anthony teaches at the Children's Arts Center at Taos Pueblo. His wife, Annie Cota Reyna, died in 1993.

Some things have changed at Taos pueblo over the years. Some things never change. Tony is grateful for what abides: "We are very fortunate to be here. We have the water, the mountains, the land, the creatures, and the game that provides food. You have to give thanks that you have good eyes to see the beauty around us. My people were farmers long before the coming of the white man. We had irrigation; we grew crops. In my day, there was no money involved. We would trade in town for what we needed. Now, it's all cash basis."

Tony sums up his beliefs with the thought: "Do what you think is right to help other people, without expecting recognition."

"To live in a community, you have to have a purpose. You have to give back, be involved and concerned, and you have to care."

—*Tony Reyna*

Gregorita Rodriguez

CURANDERA

"ALL *CURANDERAS* WORK THEIR HEALING differently from one another, but they share the faith that a greater power is working through them," said Gregorita Rodriguez. "Their patients sense this and share in the faith in the healer's source of power. I can't tell someone exactly how to heal. I can share the skills and techniques of massage of the stomach. I can explain the healing properties of the herbs. This knowledge is important, but the rest is not something you hear with your ears or see with your eyes."*

Gregorita was the first-born daughter of Ramona and Rafael Montoya. Born in 1901 in her father's house on Montoya Hill in Santa Fe, she was instructed in the art of healing by her *Tía* (Aunt) Valentina. In her father's family, one woman of each generation was selected to become a *curandera*. Valentina, who had learned healing from her mother, took Gregorita with her when she went to care for the sick and deliver babies, teaching her how to use massage and native herbs for healing.

As a child and throughout her life, Gregorita gathered herbs in Pacheco Canyon northeast of Santa Fe, where she spent her summers at El Quelites, the ranch her father homesteaded in the early 1900s. Near the Santa Fe Ski Basin, El Quelites was so named for the wild spinach that grew there. Gregorita was almost eleven when New Mexico became the forty-seventh state on January 6, 1912, and she vividly remembers wondering if the world was coming to an end. "There wasn't any warning when suddenly a terrible noise came up from the city. The church bells rang. Train whistles blew, sirens wailed, and fireworks exploded in broad daylight. . . . We had never heard so much noise."*

Gregorita's dream of becoming a nun and giving her life to God was not to be; instead, she married Manuel Rodriguez on August 7, 1922. Those were hard times. She had sixteen pregnancies; only eight of her babies survived infancy.

Although Gregorita was busy raising her children, Valentina insisted that she make time for healing. Before Valentina died, she gave Gregorita the healing book that had been given to her by her mother. One day one of Valentina's patients arrived at Gregorita's doorstep seeking help for a back ailment. Gregorita didn't feel ready to take over for her aunt, but the ailing man wouldn't leave. So Gregorita applied compresses to his back, massaged it with liniment, placed a band around his waist, and gave him herbs for his baths.

As time passed, others came. "It was always a surprise when the patients got so much better," Gregorita said. "I had the feeling that *Tía* was still looking over my shoulder."*

Gregorita went on to earn a massage diploma and in 1974 was named "Mrs. Senior Citizen of New Mexico" by Governor Bruce King. In this role, she served as an envoy, traveling throughout the state.

---

*From *Singing for My Echo* by Edith Powers (Santa Fe, N.M. : Cota Editions, 1987).

"I can explain the healing properties of herbs . . . but the rest is something your heart and spirit discover."*   —*Gregorita Rodriguez*

Helene Ruthling

FROM THE BLACK FOREST TO TESUQUE

HELENE RUTHLING CAME TO SANTA FE as a governess, and stayed to open a famous nursery school and a unique toy store. She settled in Tesuque, where the trees reminded her of her native Black Forest. Her life touched that of many legendary figures in local history, from Mabel Dodge Luhan, who employed her, to Will Shuster creator of Zozobra — the giant gloomy gus of a puppet burned at the annual Fiesta de Santa Fe — who enjoyed her boundless hospitality. Shuster was married (for the second time) in Helene's Tesuque house

Born to Carl and Frieda Maurer in 1903 in Stuttgart, Germany, Helene was an only child. In 1913, to escape the Kaiser's Army, Carl, a cabinetmaker, emigrated to Buffalo, New York. "He did beautiful inlaid work," Helene recalled. Helene and her mother, Frieda, were expected to emigrate too, but the war in Europe erupted. Unable to join "Grandpa," Frieda and Helene went to Switzerland, where Helene completed training as a children's nurse.

Helene was seventeen and spoke little English when she and her mother arrived in Buffalo in 1920. Helene did tatting in a hat shop, "which she hated," according to her daughter, Theo, and was later employed as a governess by some of Buffalo's wealthiest families. In 1928, she came to Santa Fe from Buffalo with the John Evans family. In New Mexico, Helene was governess to the grandchildren of Taos personality Mabel Dodge Luhan.

Helene married Paul Ruthling in Santa Fe in 1931. Their daughter was christened Theodora Doodlet Tesuque by Will Shuster. Twin boys, Carleton and Fordyce, completed the family. The marriage did not last, and Helene found herself looking for a way to support her three children.

How Helene raised her children was the subject of a 1952 episode of TV's *This is Your Life* hosted by Ralph Edwards. Resourceful Helene established a children's ranch, Rancho Arroyo, in Tesuque. She began by taking care of her own and friends' children. Soon word of the children's ranch spread and enrollment increased rapidly. The children at the ranch included everyone from "the Hope diamond girl to a boy with such severe emotional problems that his family was in desperate need," Theo recalls. "Helen will care for him," parents were told. Children who had stayed at the ranch returned frequently in later years, to see their "second mother."

Helene was known for her hospitality, and parties at Rancho Arroyo were community events. "Ma gave wonderful birthday parties every spring and fall. In the spring, she would celebrate Carl and Ford's birthdays while the apple trees were blooming. In the fall, when the apples were ready and the cider was pressed, we'd celebrate my birthday. Everyone in town was invited. That was just the way it was," Theo reminisced.

Mother and daughter became business partners when they opened Doodlet's; originally a Christmas shop, the emporium is known for unique, handcrafted treasures—from antiques to amusements. "We were able to get things that nobody else had because of my mother's ties with the Black Forest," Theo explains. "I don't know how she did it, but she had contacts with craftspeople throughout Germany." Forty-one years later, the shop is one of the oldest businesses in Santa Fe operated by the original owner.

"I started taking care of other children because I wanted to take care of mine—to support them, be sure that they had companion-ship, and to try to teach them cooperative living."

—Helene Ruthling

Amalia Sanchez

FIRST FIESTA QUEEN

MUCH OF SANTA FE'S COLORFUL HISTORY is reflected in the life of Amalia Sanchez. Forever known as the first Fiesta Queen, in 1927, the year she was crowned, she was thirty-five years old, married to lawyer Manuel Sanchez, and the mother of two daughters. Dana Johnson, then the editor of the *New Mexican*, originated the idea of a queen to reign over the Fiesta Parade, then known as Pasatiempo. When she learned she had been chosen, Amalia said, "Oh, you're out of your mind. I have two little children." Johnson replied, "So did Queen Victoria."

Born in 1892, Amalia grew up in the Palace Avenue home now known as Sena Plaza, a member of the seventh generation of her family to occupy that site. The historic residence we know today was built by her grandfather, Major José Sena, in 1861. "It was like a *placita*," she recalls. "My grandmother lived on the east side; we lived on the west. But there were no children to play with. We had to make our own good times."

Amalia has warm memories of childhood summers spent in her grandfather's summer home in Tesuque, where the foundry Shidoni is now located. "They were some of the happiest days of my life," she says. "There was a chapel there but no priest in Tesuque. The trees are still there. Our friends were all from the pueblos."

When the influenza epidemic of 1918 struck, Amalia was teaching elementary school. She organized a soup kitchen so those who were well could cook and bring food to those who were sick. After teaching at Manderfield School for two years, she married Manuel Sanchez at Immaculate Conception in Albuquerque and traveled with her new husband, an engineer, to the Guggenheim mines outside Chihuahua. There she became bored with only her needlework to occupy her and went to work as a teacher's aide in the village school. The activities of Pancho Villa drove the Sanchezes home to Santa Fe, where Manuel studied law and opened his practice in 1924. They built a home on Garcia Street in 1922, where Amalia lived the rest of her life.

In Santa Fe, she became a community leader, active in the Red Cross, the Women's Board of the Museum of New Mexico, the Catholic Maternity Institute, and the Federation of Republican Women. She founded La Tiendita to sell used clothing for charity and operated the thrift shop in a room where the La Fonda Hotel parking lot now stands. Earlier, she apprenticed as a milliner in Miss Mugler's shop on San Francisco Street. She is also a lifelong parishoner of St. Francis Cathedral and the mother of four.

As Fiesta Queen, Amalia wore her mother's heavy white brocaded satin wedding gown with a seven-yard train, edged with "priceless lace." She remembers the occasion well. "La Fonda was jammed. I didn't see a place where there weren't people. Then we came down, and Governor Dillon and I led the grand march all around the plaza." After he crowned her, she remembers, "I danced with the governor."

"I hate the word *Hispanic*. We are all Americans. We were born in America, though our family came from Spain."   —*Amalia Sanchez*

Gloria Sawtell

INDEFATIGABLE VOLUNTEER

GLORIA SAWTELL, ONE OF SANTA FE'S MOST ACTIVE VOLUNTEERS, first came to Santa Fe with her family in 1928. She was only three years old. "My parents loved Santa Fe," said the native of Omaha, Nebraska. "We visited for a month every summer, until World War II."

Following her graduation from Stanford University and marriage, Gloria intended to share her love of Santa Fe with her husband, Bill. The couple came to Santa Fe on their wedding trip, spending their honeymoon at Bishop's Lodge.

Finally, after years of volunteer service in Omaha, where she worked with special needs children in Junior League efforts, and later became director of the Omaha Volunteer Bureau, Gloria moved permanently to Santa Fe in 1972 with her husband Bill. She joined the League of Women Voters, serving as president for two years, then began the Volunteer Involvement Service. She served on the board of the Opera Guild, then became a founding board member of the Santa Fe Community Foundation, working in this capacity for over a decade. She has also been a program chairman for Leadership Santa Fe, a nine-month training session for those who wish to become involved with Santa Fe civic activities sponsored by the Chamber of Commerce, as well as a volunteer at the Museum of New Mexico.

"In 1982, when the Community Foundation started, it was a new concept," she said. "The purpose, to develop large resources of endowed funds, with the income invested in a diversity of projects"—education, arts, parks, for example—persuaded her the organization could make a significant contribution to Santa Fe.

Another of her activities was the New Mexico Citizens Bee, an event where senior citizens compete on their knowledge of civics, the Bill of Rights, the Constitution, and other aspects of government. She is the mother of two children.

Gloria's early and lifelong love of Santa Fe influenced many other decisions in her life. In college, she studied Spanish and Latin American affairs; when she traveled, it was to Spain and Mexico. These and other experiences somehow brought her closer to the City Different.

"One of my early memories is taking a horse trip from Pecos to Santa Fe. We rode our horses down Canyon Road, and the people came out and cheered. It was October. We went to La Fonda, and there was a fire in the big fireplace."

She cherishes memories of early Fiestas, where the entire community came out, walked in parades carrying candles, and greeted each other on the plaza, where there would be a merry-go-round. "The place was so alive!" she recalled.

"Volunteering, for me, is a wonderful way to meet new people, to learn new attitudes, and to understand other cultures."   —*Gloria Sawtell*

Jay Scherer

SELFLESS HEALER AND TEACHER

"I HAVEN'T HAD ANY REGULAR DISEASES," said eighty-year-old Jay Victor Scherer, a doctor who has devoted his life to healing others. Jay began treating people at the age of seven. Because his mother was a healer, "whenever anybody got hurt at school, they would come running to me," he said, "there was more cooperation between professions back then."

He was born in 1907 near Spokane, Washington, in a little village called Uniontown. Jay's entire family was trained in the Rudolf Steiner system, a prescribed method of self-discipline whereby a cognitive experience of the spiritual world can be achieved. His mother was a graduate of the Rudolf Steiner School in Germany. "She knew a lot about herbs and healing," and worked in the famous Dr. Foster Clinic in Idaho as Jay was growing up. "My mother had inner vision. She could look at a person and see what was wrong with them by watching the health aura," Jay said.

His father was a farmer who owned a livery stable and worked as a United States marshal. He was also an organizer. "I got my ability to organize from him. I learned a lot about how to work with people from him," Jay said. While growing up, Jay rode horseback until his father "bought the first automobile that came to town."

When Jay was six, his mother sat him down and said, "'Now Jay, I want you to make up your mind on what you really want to do with the rest of your life,'" Jay said. He wanted to be a minister, he told her, and he wanted to have a healing school.

In 1928, Jay went to Houston and studied for four years at the Dr. DePalma School of Naturopathy. While in Houston, he was ordained as a minister after completing studies at Glad Tidings in Mt. Pleasant, Texas. He later went to England to the Bainbridge Forrest School of Naturopathy, where he received degrees in naturopathy, botanic medicine, and philosophy.

Jay went to Los Angeles in the 1930s. Movie stars were his patients. In 1938 he was drafted. After joining the reserves, he moved to New Mexico. When World War II started, Jay was assigned to the Manhattan Project in Los Alamos, where he spent five years managing scientific equipment for one of the laboratories. "When the war was over, I opened the first spa in Santa Fe in 1952," he said. A pioneer in holistic health, in 1953 he established the Niagara Health Center and began to teach massage—the first massage school in New Mexico. Then in 1979 he opened Dr. Jay Victor Scherer's Academy of Natural Healing, which offered in-depth courses in massage therapy and related healing arts.

Jay never married. "My mother told me a long time ago not to get married because doctors' wives are the most neglected people in the world. Your practice comes first," he said.

Of his medical philosophy, Jay says: "I don't diagnose the ordinary man. I observe and recognize certain conditions, but I don't try to label people. I don't try to evaluate. I just absolutely know that the power of God can take care of anything."

"Most of my trouble has come from not getting enough sleep . . . because when I see a need, I take care of it." —*Jay Scherer*

SCORE

GUIDING NEW BUSINESSES

W HEN PEOPLE IN SANTA FE ARE THINKING about opening a new business, there is a place they can turn for legal, financial, and logistical advice. Thanks to the expertise of the volunteers of SCORE—the Service Corps of Retired Executives—free, high-quality business advice is available to anyone in need of it.

When D. C. "Pete" Mathewson retired to Santa Fe after a thirty-five-year career as an executive with ALCOA, after working with the city on economic development he established the Santa Fe SCORE chapter. It became part of a national network of 500 chapters with over 12,000 volunteer business counselors. About 22 SCORE counselors now work out of an office in the federal courthouse in Santa Fe.

"We try to help people with ideas," says Pete. "We orient them on matters such as licensing, state taxes, and worker's comp. We also help them write a business plan and make cash flow projections, so they can go into a bank and have a serious meeting. We explain potential sources of financing and counsel them on the location of their facility." In addition to business counseling, SCORE presents seminars of interest to people who want to start a business.

And SCORE's activities also benefit the volunteers themselves, who feel they have found the perfect "retirement" job—it's part-time, it allows them the freedom to pursue their other interests, and it provides an opportunity to give back to the community by sharing what they've learned during their years in business.

"People have ideas, but where to find sources of money is our greatest demand," says Pete. "The second biggest need is for legal counseling, and the third is for information on record-keeping."

SCORE volunteers in New Mexico work under unique conditions. The Santa Fe based group covers the northern third of the state, all the way north to Raton and all the way west to Farmington. Members can find themselves putting in long hours behind the wheel. And then there's what one member refers to as the "One of our fifty is missing" phenomenon, ie ignorance, in some quarters, of New Mexico's very existence, that can make it hard to attract venture capital to the state. Yet SCORE's successes are legion. Respecting their clients' confidentiality, the volunteers don't go around dropping names. But chances are that you've recently eaten at a restaurant or shopped at a store that opened with help from SCORE.

With so many people coming to Santa Fe with the desire to open a small Mom and Pop retail or restaurant business, the kind of information SCORE provides, and the helpful, friendly, and trustworthy way in which it is provided, is a great service to the city.

Santa Fe SCORE is able to offer advice on just about any area of business. "We cover just about everything, through one counselor or another," says Pete. The philosophy of SCORE volunteers is summed up by its founder: "We don't want to charge, we want to give."

"When you retire, you don't just want to go fishing all day. You want to keep your mind whirring."

—*SCORE Volunteer*

Bouncer Sena

AN ABIDING BELIEF IN KIDS

"I STILL SEE A LOT OF KIDS WHEN I GO to the grocery store. What should have been a two-minute errand turns into an hour," said Bouncer Sena. Bouncer's "kids" are his former students, who stop to talk with the man who was vice principal of Santa Fe High School for nearly twenty-five years.

Born John Sena to Abran and Elena Sena in Santa Fe in 1927, Bouncer was the youngest of eight children. "I was a little guy, about eleven, when one of the guys said, 'You know, you're getting to look more like a bouncer every day.' The name stuck," said Bouncer.

Bouncer grew up "on Agua Fria Street, right down from the Guadalupe Church," and attended Guadalupe School. "My father was a professional politician and worked for the New Mexico Highway Department for many years. My mother had a real commonsense philosophy, even though she only had a third grade education." When he was a small boy, his mother was accidentally burned. "During the time that she was indisposed, we never made a meal. Santa Fe was a community that cared for one another," he said.

"We are true Spaniards," said Bouncer. "My great-grandfather was a blacksmith and stood six feet, five inches and weighed 280 pounds. My cousin, Maria Isabel Sena, traced the family name. Sena derived from the River Seine."

Bouncer likes to see people keeping the Santa Fe traditions alive. "I'm a Catholic, and I believe in a lot of the things we do—the procession, Fiesta de Santa Fe," he said. "When we were little, during the day of Fiesta, my mom and dad would spend the day visiting with people they hadn't seen all year long. And then we'd go have a full meal for seventy-five cents."

Bouncer made the Santa Fe High School football team when he was a sophomore. "We had a lot of luck that year and won the state championship," he said. After graduation, Bouncer attended the University of New Mexico, but he returned home when the College of Santa Fe opened and earned a degree in business administration in 1951.

Bouncer was coaching the Demons' sophomore basketball team when he met Bernadette Ortiz. "She came to watch the games," he said. They married in 1958 and became parents to Dolores, Melinda, José, and Rebecca.

During his thirty-three years at Santa Fe High School, he "was involved in every facet of the high school—home economics, drama, debate, and junior-senior prom," Bouncer said. "I never appreciated my bilingualism until I traveled to Mexico and Spain. I spoke Spanish as master of ceremonies for the Demon band's performances abroad." In collaboration with the Santa Fe Chamber of Commerce, Bouncer created a Career Days program at the school, which received an award from the Santa Fe Community Foundation. "One of the things that I wanted to do was to let the community know what the schools are doing. Then, I wanted the schools to know how the community feels we are doing," said Bouncer.

Bouncer shared his educational philosophy. "Working with kids was the number one priority, which is as it should be. I'd spend ten to twelve hours at the school. When the kids were there, I was there."

Active in politics, Bouncer was a county commissioner from 1977 to 1980 and was involved in setting up Santa Fe's water board. "My concern was that we not grow beyond our resources," he said. "A lot of people don't think that far. I've got grandkids. We've got to think about them."

"Working with kids was the number one priority, which is as it should be."

—*Bouncer Sena*

Phil Shultz

MENDER OF BROKEN WINGS

KNOWN AS "THE BIRD MAN OF TESUQUE," Phil Shultz, a surgeon now retired, expanded his practise to include wild birds. Assisted by his wife Joanne, a surgical nurse, he performed many, many "bird operations." At least half the creatures — orphaned, poisoned, wounded by gunshot or traps—brought to him, recovered sufficiently to be released back into the wild.

Phil's interest in birds, particularly birds of prey, began in his youth. Born in Stanton, Virginia, in 1917, educated at the University of Virginia, he served as a surgeon for the army in the European theater during World War II. In college, a friend brought two young peregrine falcons to school, and Phil worked with him, helping him fly his birds.

After the war, Phil held an appointment at the American University in Beirut, and had the opportunity to observe falconry in the Middle East. Upon returning to the States, he went to practice on the Navajo Reservation at Ft. Defiance, Arizona, and there took care of injured birds with the help of some Hopis who were accustomed to caring for eagles.

While in Los Alamos, where he practiced from 1952 to 1975, Phil began rehabilitating wounded birds with the help of his sons, Albert and Eric. During the 1960s, he became active in the movement to protect and restore endangered species of birds. He was the second successful breeder of prairie falcons in captivity.

His interest in wild birds, as well as his wide travels and rugged adventures backpacking in places like the Galapagos Islands, East Africa, and the Alaskan outback led Phil to positions on the boards of the Sierra Club and the Nature Conservancy. A firm believer in "the active physical life," for many years he took twenty mile hikes in the Santa Fe area every Wednesday with a group of friends known as the "Santa Fe Chile and Marching Society."

When Phil moved to Tesuque in 1956 he built enclosures to house the wounded creatures. Hundreds of raptors, some brought in by his sons, some by state and federal fish and game officials, some by the Audubon Society, some sent from Texas and Colorado, passed through his hands.

Over time, he learned to understand the needs of each bird. "Ospreys and bald eagles are irascible, while golden eagles and falcons are quite cooperative." The greatest challenge was finding methods of feeding the raptors. After healing them, Phil would then get the birds fit for the wild once more by exercising them in falconry techniques.

Today, much of his work has been taken over by Dr. Kathleen Ramsey of the Española Wildlife Rescue Society, which heals birds and gives those that cannot be released into the wild to public education programs.

"Sixty-four golden eagles have passed through here." —*Phil Shultz*

Carol & Marcus Smith

DEDICATED DOCTORS

IN APRIL 1945 DR. MARCUS SMITH REACHED DACHAU with a team of US army officers sent to reclaim the lives of the more than 32,000 prisoners. Memories of the concentration camp outside Munich haunted the good doctor all his life."He tried to keep everything in," his wife Carol recalls,"but there were some times when he just couldn't." The disturbing memoir he published in 1972 *Dachau: The Harrowing of Hell* gives a glimpse of the kindly, practical physician, who set right to work on arrival, inventorying the camp kitchen.

Carol and Marcus Smith, she a pediatrician, he a radiologist, married in 1941 and came to live in Santa Fe in 1948. (He had been stationed here, at Bruns Army Hospital, during part of the war.) In 1951 Carol was stricken with polio while pregnant with their fourth child. Confined to a wheelchair for life, she continued to practise medicine and remained active in community affairs.

"I was lucky I was a pediatrician,"she told us, " because I could just come back and go to work. You don't have to stand up when you're talking to kids." She received care and rehab at the University of Chicago, "where there was a very positive attitude and all ther patients had jobs." While there she studied bone pathology. She was also active in child protective services, working to assist children in situations of abuse or neglect.

While Carol worked at rural clinics in Rio Arriba and Taos Counties, and as the United Mine Workers' physician at the Madrid mines, Marcus made the "milk run" to Las Vegas, Espanola and Taos. Often the state police would stop him for coffee and a report on road conditions.

Both doctors participated fully in civic life, especially with opera and concert groups. Marcus came from a musical family and enjoyed singing with the Santa Fe Chorus. In fact, Carol told us, "he would have preferred to have been an opera singer. As a young man he was offered a scholarship to study opera, but he turned it down in favor of medicine. But music was his first love."

In 1977 Marcus received a grant from the National Endowment for the Humanities to write a history of medicine and hospitals in the New Mexico territory. Illness kept him from completing the book.

The Smiths' son Andrew is an art dealer and runs the Andrew Smith Gallery of photography, on San Francisco Street.

Carol remembered her early years in Santa Fe, "We moved here because of opportunities. We moved here with a baby and a crib in our car and enough money for a downpayment on a house. We used to square dance, play bridge at the bridge club, and create a nuisance in the precinct. We worked on community projects because that's what everyone did."

"No one of us is absolutely essential. It's all a community effort."

—*Carol Smith*

Myrtle Stedman

ADOBE ARTIST

A PAINTER, A POET, AND A WRITER, Myrtle Stedman is best known for the work in adobe restoration and design she began shortly after arriving in Tesuque in 1934, with her artist husband, Wilfred Stedman.

Ina Sizer Cassidy described the remarkable Stedmans in those years "They are both artists, both good ones, and as they are united in their art as well as in matrimony they are not to be separated when writing about them. Their studio home among the apple trees on their fruit ranch at Tesuque on Highway 64 reflects this 'togetherness,' for they are that rare combination in life, fifty-fifty, partners, in their art, their home and their two small sons."*

Born in 1908, Myrtle, the daughter of a builder, met the prominent English painter, designer, and illustrator Wilfred while studying art in Houston. He was sixteen years her senior.. After they married, they transformed their ancient adobe home in the apple orchard, and built new adobe houses, which they rented to artists and writers. They also carved their own furniture and gardened, living lives of great self-sufficiency.

In 1948, Myrtle, one of the first and only licensed women contractors in New Mexico, also built the adobe home where she still resides.

With her husband, Myrtle coauthored two books on adobe restoration and design, *Adobe Architecture* and *Adobe Remodeling and Fireplaces*. Today she is recognized both as an authority on adobe and as an independent woman who struggled to maintain her own identity in marriage. She transformed her life through her writing. In her intimate autobiography *A House Not Made of Hands*, Myrtle relates how she survived the deaths of her husband, son, and other close family members by continuing to develop her individuality, her spirituality, and her relationships. She tells, too, how she built not only houses but the marriage, in which she grew from a sheltered young woman to an independent figure, who, as a widow in 1950, did the unheard of and continued living alone in her Tesuque home. A book of poems, *Of One Mind*, continues her spiritual explorations.

"When I've come across problems, when I've been stressed, I always looked for the answers to why I was experiencing those things. Asking the questions provided me with answers, which eventually led to solutions, and in those I find security," she explained her positive approach to life. **

---

* *New Mexico Magazine*, 1936.
** From John Villani, "Stedman's Book Is Chronicle of Curiosity," *New Mexican*, n.d.

"You use your mind to get whatever you want out of life, instead of what you don't want."**   —*Myrtle Stedman*

John Stephenson

FEEDING THE MULTITUDES

"THE SANTA FE COMMUNITY FARM is probably one of the oldest farms in the United States," said its founder, John Stephenson. Located on forty acres of some of the last undeveloped land in Santa Fe, "it was farmed by the Indians before the Spanish came, so it goes back a long way." The land belongs to John; the farm's entire harvest is donated to the homeless, hungry, and disabled of Santa Fe. In 1995, the Community Farm distributed almost $24,000 worth of fresh produce. Raised with the help of nearly 575 volunteers, the crops benefited more than twenty-five Santa Fe agencies.

A native Santa Fean, John was born at home to Clyde and Clara Stephenson in 1914, at 232 Paseo. "My family was from southern Iowa. They came to New Mexico for my father's health. He had tuberculosis and died when I was two."

Although he was on the small side, John played football and basketball at Santa Fe High School; there were twenty-six students in his graduating class in 1931 or 1932."

An Eagle Scout, John collaborated with Uncle Benny Hyde, the naturalist and educator whose family donated 350 acres in Little Tesuque Canyon for the creation of Hyde State Park. "We worked up there most of a summer collecting animals. We caught two porcupines and a ground squirrel. It wasn't very successful."

John attended college in California and at New Mexico State University but transferred to Colorado State University to study forestry. His first job was in Deadwood, South Dakota. In 1936 he was paid $2 per day as a member of a field crew for the Rocky Mountain Equipment Station. "Out of our graduating class, only six of us got jobs." John returned to Santa Fe when he was offered a job as a range examiner.

John met his wife, Katherine, at a school carnival. A math teacher, Katherine was from Albuquerque. They were married in Albuquerque in 1940 and raised three sons. After serving in Europe in World War II, John returned home and bought the farm in 1945. "When we bought it, it was just an idle piece of land. We built the house, drilled the wells, put up fences, and planted the orchard in about 1947," he recalled.

John retired from the Forest Service at the age of fifty-one "to avoid being transferred to the small town of Datil, New Mexico." Retirement has allowed him to focus on his farm and do a lot of volunteer work for New Vistas, Red Cross, First Presbyterian Church, the Boy Scouts, and the American Legion. "Katherine was really the person who got me doing things like the Community Farm," he said. "She was always interested in doing things that helped the community." Retirement allowed the Stephensons to travel throughout the world. John, who took up weightlifting in his seventies, competed internationally. He traveled to Perth, Australia, in 1994, and at the age of eighty finished second in the seventy kilo or under category.

"Professionals would never do it this way," John said, pointing to low branches in his orchard. "Some have been left purposefully low so that they can be harvested from the ground or by people in wheelchairs. We've had all ages and all types of people" come to work on the two acres of orchard and two acres of crops. "It's not necessarily the most efficient farm, but we're trying to serve the needs of the community."

"When I was a youngster, we used to say Santa Fe—elevation 7,000, population 7,000. . . . We used to figure 30 gallons a day of water per person; now we figure 300 gallons a day with a population of 70,000."

—*John Stephenson*

Bob Storey

INTERVIEWING AS ART

BOB STOREY HAD A HEAD START ON OTHER REPORTERS. "My dad was a lobbyist for the New Mexico Farm and Livestock Bureau for thirty-two years," he said. "In our family, books and politics, debate and expression were always a part of the family."

Born in 1947 in Las Vegas, New Mexico, and raised in Albuquerque, Bob grew up in a home where dinner guests often included New Mexico's governor, judges, and politicians. "I thought everyone had these guys to dinner," he recalled. Bob attended school in Albuquerque and graduated from Highland High School.

Bob hadn't planned to be a journalist; he wanted to be a marine biologist. But after serving a stint as editor of the University of New Mexico daily, the *Lobo,* Bob was hooked. The man who had the greatest influence on him as a journalist, as a writer, was Tony Hillerman.

In 1969, Bob was voted the outstanding senior male journalism graduate at the University of New Mexico. After a two-year hitch in the army, he moved to Santa Fe in 1972 and began working for the *New Mexican*. He spent the next sixteen years working as an editorial writer, state government political reporter, business editor, and assistant weekend editor. He covered every political campaign from 1968 to 1988. Bob "asked the hard question, and held me and other politicians he covered to a high standard of integrity. Yet he always gave credit where it was due," New Mexican Congressman Bill Richardson says. In 1983, the congressman asked Bob to accompany him and a congressional delegation to El Salvador to oversee an Easter truce in the civil war. Bob was one of the first United States journalists to be allowed to visit a political prison at a time of rampant human rights abuse.

Bob was instrumental in creating Santa Fe Community College, through his editorials in support of community education. He considered passage of the bond issue that financed the college as "the proudest moment" in his life. After he retired from journalism, Bob enrolled at Santa Fe Community College and earned a degree in computer science.

Bob met his wife, Sandy, when they both worked at the *New Mexican*. They raised a son, Anthony. "Sandy is one of the pleasures in my life because she has always supported everything that I've done. . . . It takes quite a bit for a woman to be married to a reporter who has to cover the Legislature."

In retirement Bob did public relations—as a volunteer— for the Governor's Conference on Aging. The experienced journalist shared his expertise with Living Treasures volunteers, training them in the techniques of interview and oral history.

Upon learning that he was terminally ill in his mid-forties, Bob turned his concern to the high number of Santa Fe teens who had reported thoughts of suicide. "If I were still writing editorials," he said, "I'd be right in the middle of it."*

---

*From an article by Kay Bird, *New Mexican*, October 13, 1991.

"When [other]
kids were . . .
playing cops and
robbers, . . . I
was sitting in the
State House
listening to
legislative
debates."

—*Bob Storey*

Anita Gonzales Thomas

PRESERVING SPANISH COLONIAL NEW MEXICO

"IT WASN'T UNTIL I WENT TO ST. FRANCIS Parochial School that I began to get acquainted with children who weren't relatives," said Santa Fe native Anita Gonzales Thomas. "My earliest years were on Garcia Street." Her great-grandmother "owned all the land on the 200 block of Delgado Street." Anita's grandmother gave the land she inherited to Anita's father "because he helped to support her after my grandfather died. The rest of the street was all cousins—the Bacas and the Delgados," Anita said.

Born in 1908 to Paul and Elizabeth Gonzales, Anita was the oldest of twelve children. Elizabeth was Governor Clyde Tingley's secretary of state in the 1930s.

"St. Francis Parochial School was where the La Fonda Hotel is now. When I graduated from eighth grade, I went to the all-girl Loretto Academy, a boarding and day school," Anita recalled. She graduated from Loretto Academy in 1926 and was awarded a scholarship to Loretto Heights College in Denver, Colorado. "Before I went, I had a job at the capitol because the Democrats were in. When I got back, the Republicans were in, so there wasn't a job."

Anita hadn't thought about teaching, but when she was offered a job in Cañoncito, she taught there for two years; then she returned to Santa Fe to teach fourth and fifth grades at Manderfield School.

Her future husband, Tommy Thomas, came to Santa Fe as a lieutenant in the Army Reserve. At the time, "President Roosevelt had started the Civilian Conservation Corps during the Depression," Anita said, "and there were two CCC camps in Santa Fe. I met Tommy when Father Jerome from St. Francis Cathedral went to say mass at one of the camps. I was in the cathedral choir, and Father Jerome thought it would be nice if we sang some of the Spanish songs. We were married by Father Jerome, who introduced us, on August 16, 1936."

As an officer in the Army Reserve, Tommy was called up and trained as an induction officer before World War II began. "He was sent to Phoenix, and I followed. We were in Phoenix when Pearl Harbor was attacked. I was in Phoenix when the war ended." The couple returned to Santa Fe in the spring of 1947, where Anita was asked to do substitute teaching. She later returned to full-time teaching.

Anita belonged to the Spanish Colonial Arts Society for a number of years. In 1971 she had just retired from teaching when George Paloheimo decided to open a museum of Spanish colonial life, on land he owned in La Cienega. Opened in 1972, El Rancho de las Golondrinas (The Ranch of the Swallows) is a living history museum whose purpose is to foster understanding of, respect for, and pride in the language, culture, and history of Spanish colonial New Mexico. "I didn't have money to help with the project, but I had lots of time," Anita recalled. For twenty years Anita was secretary of the Colonial New Mexico Historical Foundation, which "ran the museum until Mr. Paloheimo placed the museum into a trust."

Active in numerous civic and church organizations, Anita particularly enjoyed her work with the Old Santa Fe Association. "I was on the board for twelve years. It was during that time that the city passed the historic ordinance."

Lily Lopez

"I'm into everything. . . . I think I've always enjoyed whatever I was involved in."   —*Anita Gonzales Thomas*

Frances Tyson

ENERGY SAVER

IT'S HARD TO BE AN HONEST ENVIRONMENTALIST. Every time you flip a light switch at home, you're part of the problem. Frances Tyson is part of the solution. She lobbies tirelessly in environmental issues, and she does so from an energy efficient house.

Born in Kentucky in 1912, Frances graduated from Vassar College in 1934 with a degree in economics. In 1975, when her husband, MIT scientist and chemical engineer Wesley Tyson, was diagnosed with Alzheimer's disease, she moved with him to Santa Fe, to be closer to her family. This move opened the doorway to her future as an environmental activist.

Wesley's illness kept the couple out of their customary "social stuff, like bridge," she recalls. "So I got into what I was interested in."

What interested Frances was saving energy. In Santa Fe, she first built a solar greenhouse. After her husband's death, she moved to Las Vegas and constructed an energy-efficient house of her own design. Using a wind generator and photovoltaics, she built a home that gets heat and light from natural, renewable sources. One of her great pleasures is giving people tours of her house to show them how an environmentally conscious home can operate.

Frances's career as an environmentalist took off when she attended a conference of the New Mexico Solar Energy Group at Ghost Ranch. "There I was, with all these thirty year olds," she remembers.

Frances belongs to at least fifty environmental groups and does an enormous amount of reading in her field. She synthesizes all the information she obtains, and sends it out to the world in a very personal way—by corresponding with institutions and individuals she hopes to influence. She writes letters to colleges and public figures in an attempt to increase their awareness of environmental issues. And she actively instigates lawsuits "to shut down nuclear plants."

The issues she has decided to tackle are enormous. And her work carries enormous frustrations. Appeals go without response. Situations requiring immediate remediation, to protect the planet from further damage or danger, drag on. But Frances remains undaunted. In many ways, her activities demonstrate Gandhi's principle that "the result of the journey is not so important as the fact that you are committed to making the journey."

Frances's message to the world is, "Be responsible. Be kind. And don't blow your mind—you need it."

"I'm down to $19 a month for heat, light, pumping water from a six-hundred-foot well, the whole schmoo." —*Francis Tyson*

Pablita Velarde

ARTIST WHO LED THE WAY

The life of America's leading Indian woman artist is a story of determination and dedication winning out over daunting obstacles. You'd never guess it from her gentle paintings, full of charming narrative detail.

Born at Santa Clara Pueblo in 1918, Pablita was given the Tewa name Tse Tan, Golden Dawn. When she was five her mother died, and she herself suffered a brief bout of blindness. She was sent to St Catherines Indian School in Santa Fe, and there given the name Pablita Velarde.

Continuing her studies at the Santa Fe Indian School, she was the only girl in the painting class. "The boys were mean," she recalls. "They poked fun at me. 'cause I wanted to be an artist. You'd do better washing dishes or washing clothes or scrubbing floors, they said." And her father, Herman Velarde, "didn't believe in a woman painting pictures and not doing a woman's work or learning to make a living," so he sent her to Española to study bookkeeping and typing.

But Pablita's own talent and the encouragement of her teacher, Dorothy Dunn, and Tonita Pena, the only other Indian woman artist of the day, kept her on her chosen path. Early on, she began experimenting with earth pigments she ground herself, the way the "old ones" painted. Following graduation from the Indian School in 1936, Pablita took odd jobs to support herself, working as a maid and a nurse's aide. She taught when she could, while continuing to paint at night.

Pablita's break came when the Park Service hired her to paint murals depicting Pueblo life at Bandelier National Monument. Then, while working as a switchboard operator in Albuquerque, she met and married police officer Herbert Hardin. Following her divorce in 1957, she supported her two children, Helen and Herbert, through her painting. "I didn't really think of myself as an artist until my kids were in school, and I thought: I'm gonna compete."

While the life of Helen Hardin, a brilliant painter, ended tragically with her death at age forty-one from cancer, Herbert is now a metal sculptor who shows and sells with his mother.

While going through her divorce, "as therapy" Pablita wrote and illustrated *Old Father Story Teller*, which recounts Pueblo creation stories told to her by her father and grandmother, and so became the first Pueblo woman to publish a book. "I needed something to take the sting out and keep my mind working," she says. Later, after building her own house at Santa Clara, she took up doll making and is today a beloved storyteller as well.

"It's nice to be recognized," says Pablita, who was awarded France's Palmes des Académiques and has earned honors at Santa Fe Indian Market since the mid-1930s. Noted for their accurate and detailed depiction of Indian life, her paintings of ceremonial dances, pottery making, and winnowing wheat-which once sold for $1.50 now go for thousands of dollars.

Surrounded by her family in her modest Albuquerque home, Pablita reflects on her life. "I don't feel like I'm the greatest thing that ever happened to Mother Earth. I'm kind of a mixed-up Christian," she laughs. "I'm still a believer in both ways, Indian and Christian. If one don't hear me, the other one will. I've been blessed with faith in both worlds."

"I was always drawing. Something always was in my head that wanted to come out. Something just kept telling me: do it, do it, do it."
—*Pablita Velarde*

Charlie & Dorothy Wade

MAKING MUSIC AND CREATING GARDENS

No hay mal que por bien no venga, says the proverb. There's no ill but brings some good. Dorothy and Charlie Wade are a case in point. Poor health brought Dorothy Wade to Santa Fe in her sixties. She recovered health and energy, and planted a garden where none had been before, while her husband, a retired jazz musician, brought pleasure to Santa Fe seniors with his vast repertoire of golden oldies.

Dorothy was born in Philadelphia in 1911. Her parents were pharmacists. Painful dislocations marked her childhood. Her father was badly burned in a laboratory fire. Her mother died of tuberculosis. Her father remarried. Dorothy was raised on her stepmother's farm in upstate New York. She received her primary education in one-room schoolhouses.

She wanted to be a dancer, but her father wouldn't hear of it. Teacher or nurse were the approved alternatives. In the late 1920s she taught kindergarten to children at risk of tuberculosis, "outdoors all winter, in the snow and the rain," she recalled. "They were dressed for it... that was what they did in those days...fresh air, fluids, rest and sunshine."

In New York City, she met a musician and "chased him all over town and finally got him." That was Charley Wade, born in Fall River in 1904, into a musical family. "We had a family quartet. I was the fifth wheel." At four, he began to sing popular songs, "not good, but loud." Decades later, he still played those old standards. He won a scholarship to the New England Conservatory of Music, but left to seek fame and fortune in the Big Apple.

"New York was especially valuable because it was the starting point of the radio networks—the big network shows of which I did one, the Bell Telephone Hour, for twenty-five years," he recalled. During World War II, he joined the Artie Shaw Band and performed at Guadalcanal.

Health problems convinced Dorothy to move to Santa Fe in the 1970s, as her doctor recommended a high, dry climate. She brought her love of gardening and Charlie brought his love of music to their retirement community, and continued to enjoy each other's company. "We got along together, which is what you want, someone that is amiable," Charlie remarked.

"The garden at the Santuario de Guadalupe was just a patch of weeds when I came here," Dorothy recalled. Focusing on the theme "Plants of the Bible," and using her special compost for soil, Dorothy, an organic gardener, planted a garden with many flowers, shrubs, and flowering herbs native to the Holy Land. The garden at the historic church received national recognition, and Dorothy received the May Duff Walters Trophy for Preservation of Beauty from the National Council of Federated Garden Clubs.

Charlie loved to give jazz concerts. He got interested in making Indian flutes, and learned to play native American music. He played on the plaza, for the Open Hands program for the elderly, and at nursing homes. He enjoyed playing requests at the former O. J. Sarah's and Winery restaurants. "I've always had a good memory for tunes," he said. "I found a list of 125 tunes people like most. I memorized 100. Then I memorized another 500, just to be on the safe side."

"I really kicked
around all over
the place and
played music all
my life."
—*Charlie Wade*

Sallie Wagner

GUARDIAN OF CULTURAL HERITAGE

THERE ARE NO HOWLING COYOTES in Sallie Wagner's home. Instead, there are boxes full of *nacimientos* (nativities) from the pueblos and the Spanish villages, and a Japanese door curtain over the door depicting animals coming to the Buddha. "'The art of the craftsman is a bond between the peoples of the world,' says a sign above the Folk Art Museum," said Sallie, who has collected and marketed Native American and folk art throughout her life.

Born in 1913 to Dwight and Elsie Wagner in "West, by God, Virginia," Sallie grew up with a brother and sister in Wheeling. "We had quite a bit of property. My brother kept finding arrowheads and grinding stones all over the property," she said. When he got tired of his collection, he gave it to Sallie. "I became interested in Indians through that. One Sunday afternoon I was reading the travel section of the *New York Times*, and I read all about New Mexico—about the Indians out here. I talked my father into bringing me out; that was in 1928," said Sallie. "I kept coming back."

Dwight Wagner was in the steel business. "The company owned a lot of flat land along the Ohio River" on which they planned to build mills, Sallie said. "There were a lot of mounds on that land. I persuaded my father to have the company sponsor a dig on one of the mounds, and the Pennsylvania Museum did a dig one summer. I think I was about fourteen years old, but they let me dig anyway," and the anthropologists suggested to Sallie that she consider attending the University of Chicago. After completing boarding school in Washington, D.C., Sallie went to Chicago and began her studies. She returned to Santa Fe during the summers.

Sallie met William Lippincott at college. "He got a job with the National Park Service. We got married in 1936," she said. While working at Canyon de Chelly, William decided to leave government employment. The couple bought Wide Ruins Trading Post in 1938.

"Wide Ruins was seventeen miles north of Chambers," Arizona, said Sallie. "The nearest town was Gallup—seventy miles away." Wide Ruins was a general store, and William and Sallie sold "everything from wagons to lollipops," she said. "I don't think there are any trading posts anymore. It's all based on a cash economy now." Sallie and her husband were in the trading post business for thirteen years, and during that time she persuaded Navajo rug makers to use vegetable dyes.

William and Sallie returned to Santa Fe in the early 1950s. William was director of the Museum of International Folk Art from 1954 to 1957. "This was before Indian things and folk art became so popular," Sallie said. "I undertook to try to make those things more popular and more accessible. I spent most of my days going around to the Indian and Spanish villages, simply buying anything that I thought was good, and paying for it right then and there." She'd ship her finds to stores in the United States and Europe. Just about the time Sallie got tired and decided she couldn't continue, "there was an upsurge in interest."

Sallie then took on such tasks as identifying and organizing the photographs in the archives of the Museum of New Mexico. She is a founding member of the Archeological Society of America and is a fellow of the School of American Research in Santa Fe.

Judith M. Liersch

"I'm very interested in folk art, and I like going to places where that is still being done." —*Sallie Wagner*

Corinne Wolfe

LOBBYING FOR HUMAN RIGHTS

"I HAVE ALWAYS BEEN INVOLVED WITH CHILDREN," says Corinne Wolfe. "From the very early days of the Depression [I was] concerned with families, children, and the elderly. Some of my first work as a social worker was in adoptions and foster care."

Born Corinne Howell in El Paso, Texas, in 1912, she was the eldest of five children. Her father was a cattleman, and she grew up on a ranch in the Sacramento Mountains near Alamogordo, New Mexico. "My father was a very just man. . . . He had great feeling that everyone should be respected, and each person should have his own rights," she said.

Corinne went to high school and college in El Paso at the Texas College of Mines and Metallurgy. She was sixteen when she began college. "When I went, they were just starting to make it a liberal arts school," she said, "I didn't know anything about social work at the time." But she learned about it from a sociology teacher in her "junior or senior year in college."

Corinne earned a teaching certificate, but she never used it. "In the 1930s, it was the beginning of the Depression, and there was incredible need. I first started working in 1933 with the El Paso Employment and Rehabilitation Division. That was when the transients were beginning to come across the state. I helped run a transient bureau."

From 1934 to 1935 Corinne went to Tulane University to work on her master's degree, and then returned to Texas, where she held a number of social work jobs until after World War II. "After the war, I went to Fort Worth to work at the Veterans Administration, trying to work out the care of wounded veterans coming back," Corinne said.

Corinne married Howard Wolfe, an accountant, in 1936. When she divorced, Corinne moved to San Francisco to work for the Department of Health, Education and Welfare. In the 1950s and 1960s, Corinne went to Washington, D.C., to work in the Bureau of Public Assistance, a job that took her throughout the world. "The first visit that I made was to the Soviet Union. I spent two months there studying their social security system," she said. "I've been to Denmark and Sweden. I've been to most of the developing countries; I've been to Iran, Israel, to Japan, India, and China. . . . One of my specialties in Japan was teaching participatory management."

By the time Corinne left Washington in 1972, she was head of the Social and Rehabilitation Service's Office of Research and Training, "which covered public assistance, child welfare, aging, vocational rehabilitation, and juvenile delinquency," she said.

After moving to New Mexico in 1972, Corinne was instrumental in developing social work programs at Highlands University, the College of Santa Fe, and New Mexico State University. She was also a principal plaintiff in a successful lawsuit filed to force the state to improve its services to children in foster care. "One of the problems is that children stay in foster care too long," she said. "The basis of the suit [was] to get children into permanent homes as quickly as possible."

Honored as the 1986 Social Worker of the Year by the National Association of Social Workers, Corinne spends her golden years lobbying city and state governments on behalf of social service programs. In retirement, she found, "I can say what I want, and still continue to work."

"I graduated
from college
when I was
nineteen. I've
been working
ever since."

—*Corinne Wolfe*

K. Rose Wood

ADVOCATE FOR SENIORS

NEW MEXICANS OF ALL AGES owe a vote of thanks to K. Rose Wood, founder and first director of the State Agency on Aging. Under her guidance and leadership, the organization that began in 1967 as the Governor's Commission on Aging evolved into a full-fledged agency, providing services for all New Mexico seniors.

She was born in Chicago in 1905. She started out as a social worker in Minnesota. The Depression brought her to New Mexico in 1935. She began her long career in state government at the Departments of Social Welfare and Public Health. In 1959, "after working a lot of the elderly through the welfare set-up, she thought, 'Why not start something exclusively for our seniors?'"Her vision was realized in 1967 with the passage of federal legislation creating commissions on aging throughout the U.S.

In 1965, after helping write the bill that created the state commission on aging, K. Rose had two primary goals: first, to make the organization visible; and second, to get a healthy budget and staff.

"I dreamed about it," she recalled. "I read all the laws in the other states to find out what would work well for us. I had to learn; it took a long time."

In the course of studying gerontology, watching her own mother and other relatives age, and finally, in 1976, retiring and assuming a busy schedule of volunteer work, K. Rose developed her own positive philosophy of aging.

"I watch fantastic things being done by older people in art, in literature, in architecture. These are ageless benefits. No sense in deploring [aging], no sense in worrying about it. You don't despair when you're alive. Life is good, and you stay with that part."

An unabashed cat lover, K. Rose lived alone with her pets, after the death of her husband, Charlie Wood, in 1965. "I have my own place. It's got peace and quiet, it's like a sanctuary. I have never felt alone. I don't think people are alone."

In retirement she continued to serve on national and district boards. And K. Rose corresponded with some forty people and spent time "learning about other people's religion and cultures." She defined society's problem, "We don't understand the other guy, and so we hate him. We go to war with him because he's different."

A strong advocate for the elderly, K. Rose maintained, "The seniors of the state need more organizations and more unity to make sure of acquiring more dignity and independence."

"Everybody's going to get old. You might as well be happy and pleasant about it. There are ways of aging without falling apart."

–K. Rose Wood

Thank You

LIST OF DONORS

We are grateful to our wonderful donors who believed in this project and made it happen.

Kathy, Rick & Liza Abeles
Herman Agoyo
Hope Aldrich
James & Peyton Auerbach
Burch & Florence Ault
Ballen & Company
The Bank of Santa Fe
Rutgers & Leslie Barclay
Martha Bateman
Charles & Diana Bell
Lisa Bemis
Betty Berchtold
Alice Ann Biggerstaff
Elspeth Bobbs
Lowell & Sarah Boles
James Borders
Michael & Susan Boyle
Eleanor Broh-Kahn
Wiley T. Buchanan III
Dorothy Bunting
Tish Butler
Capitol City Title Services, Inc. &
    LaMerle Boyd
Robert & Patricia Cardinale
Kay Carlson
Center for Study of Community
Mona L. Coffield

Cecelia Conley
Kay Coughlin
Community Bank
Barbara Conroy
Kenneth Dahl
Nancy Dahl
Ann Dasburg
Kay Davis
Stanley & Zu Davis
Davis & Associates
Connie Dempsey
Walter & Barbara Drew
Phil Edgerton & Gayle Maxon
Anne Hays Egan
Marjorie Miller-Engel
Dane Ericson
Carl & Norma Evans
Robert & Ellyn Feldman
First State Bank
Kathryn Flynn
Robert & Denise Ford
Michael & Pat French & Family
Jim & Pat Fries
Victoria Frigo
Reese & Anne Fullerton
Jesus Carlos Galvan
Zannie Garcia

Eric & Elise Gent
Girard Construction Company
Glenna Goodacre
Peter Goodwin
Nancy Graham
Dean & Ginny Graves
Gregory Green & Shirley Scott
Shirley Greene
Nan Newton & Dave Grusin
Jean Hafemann
Michael Gold & Darlene Hall
Edward T. Hall
Jim, Tim & Jon Hall
Glenna Halverson-Boyd
Barbara Harrelson
Ruth Hashimoto
Leon & Rosalie Heller
Nancy Herrick
John Hiatt & Margret Carde
Michael Hice
Larry & Susan Higbie
Historic Santa Fe Foundation
Houser Family
Philip Howell
Craig M. Huitfeldt & Jane Smith
    Huitfeldt
Cornelia Hull

Jackalope & Darby McQuade
Allen L. Jennings
Michael & Susan Jepson
Diane Jergins
Bill & Lu Johnson
Christine H. Johnson
Bill & Peggy Jones
Leonard & Kathleen Katz
Cristina Kenney
Jim & Sudie Kirkpatrick
Stephanie Kosicki
Sally Kruse
Mary Kuelthau
Leslie La Kind
Bruce & Mary Anne Larsen
Robert & Joyce Libutti
Judith M. Liersch
Ramón & Nance López & Family
Arlene LewAllen
Conchita López
Los Alamos National Bank
Pauline Lujan
Bill & Norma Lumpkins
David & Susan Mackie
Virginia F. Mackie
Barbara Vogt Mallery
Matteucci Fenn Galleries
Marvin & Naomi Mattis
James & Susan Mayer
Dominique Mazeaud
Duncan & Molly McBranch
Taylor McConnell
McCune Charitable Foundation &
    Owen Lopez
Shirley McNally
Larry Adelaide Meyer
Virginia Miller
Charles & Edwina Milner
Tom & Shirley Minett
Modrall, Sperling, Roehl & Sisk, P.A.
The Mortgage Company & C. Easterwood

Nicholas & Annette Molnar
Bernardo & Catherine Monserrat
Lola Moonfrog
Ann Morgan
The Mortgage Company & C.
    Easterwood
Larom B. Munson
Lloyd Kiva New
Christi Newhall
The New Mexican
Deanne K. Newman
Miller & Jeannette Nichols
Lewis Nightingale
Charles Northrup
Norwest Bank New Mexico, N.A.-
    Santa Fe
Office Depot & Judith Rogala
Sandra Oriel
Owings Dewey Company
Pauline Patraw
Bill & Alice Peden
PEO Sisterhood, Chapter F
Dorothy Perron
Gene Petchesky
Kathleen Peters
Rod & Claire Peterson
Dickie Pfaelzer
Deede Phillips
Margaret Phinney
Geral & Yara Pitchford
Pauline Pollock
Hugh & Gayle Prather
Theo Raven
Philippe Register
Bill & Barbara Richardson
Mara Robinson
Rosemary Romero
Ronald Ross
Ford Ruthling
Jack & Lou Ryan
Sanbusco Market Center & Joe Schepps

Santa Fe Abstract Ltd., Walter S. Duran, Pres.
Gloria Sawtell
Dr. Jay Scherer's Academy of Natural
    Healing
Curtis Schwartz
Douglas W. Schwartz
Juanita Sena
Katherine Shelton
Jane Shea
Mary Ann Shaening
Philip L. Shultz
Elliot Skinner & Linda Hibbs
Andrew Smith, Inc.
Myrtle Stedman
Faith Strong
Susan Seedman
Sunwest Bank
Nancy Terry
Territorial Abstract & Title Co.
Anita Thomas
Kathryn Tillson
Mary Timkin
Frances Tyson
Jan Unna & Anne Murray
Vic Vandegriff
Wadle Galleries
Sallie Wagner
Karen T. Walker
Mary Walton
Stephen Watkins
Claire Weber
Sol & Marsha Wiener
Yvonne Wilson
Nancy Meem Wirth
Nancy Witter
Witter Bynner Foundation for Poetry &
    Steven Schwartz
Keith & Letta Wofford
Corinne Wolfe

About the Authors

The Photographer

JOANNE RIJMES: Received her MA in photography, Illinois Institute of Technology. Her work is in the permanent collections of the Art Institute of Chicago and the Baltimore Museum of Art, where she also had a one person exhibit, as well as other collections. Her work has appeared in publications across the United States. She lives in Dulce, New Mexico. Her photography for this book spans the first ten years of the Living Treasure program.

The Project Founder

MARY LOU COOK (AKA MLC): Calligrapher, author, teacher, minister, and community peace worker. As founder of the Living Treasures she has been its steady source of energy and heart. She has received numerous international, national, and community honors as a distinguished leader.

The Writers

KAREN NILSSON BRANDT: An award-winning journalist for the Los Alamos Monitor, novelist, freelance writer, and, for twenty years, a social worker. She is presently writing a book based on her work for the Manhattan Project Reunion and her own lifetime experiences on "The Hill."

SHARON NIEDERMAN: Author of award-winning "A Quilt of Words," "Shaking Eve's Tree," and recently released cookbook "Hellish Relish." She taught college English and Women's Studies at Metropolitan State College, Denver, and now lives in Albuquerque. She is a frequent contributor to national and regional magazines and newspapers.